AI in Education –
An Academic Revolution

By Dr. Sarit J. Levy

Table of Contents

Dedication:

To my father, Eddie Levy, whose wisdom and steadfast guidance have been a cornerstone in my life. The echo of your voice, ever-present in my thoughts, has profoundly influenced my strategic business decisions, scholarly publications, and the core of my heart. Through your perspective, I navigate life's complexities, ensuring my endeavors are aligned with integrity and purpose. This book is a testament to your enduring influence, reflecting the values and principles you have instilled in me. With deepest gratitude and love, I dedicate this work to you.

Prologue

The triumph of the future of education stands on the brink of a revolution driven by the relentless advancement of artificial intelligence (AI) despite its vintage caliber heritage. The integration of AI into educational systems promises not merely an evolution but a transformation of learning paradigms. From personalized learning paths to intelligent tutoring systems, AI is reshaping how we perceive and engage with education. This book, "AI in Education: An Academic Revolution," embarks on a comprehensive exploration of AI's profound impact on education. It delves into the historical context, current implementations, and future possibilities of AI in various educational settings.

As educators, policymakers, and learners, we find ourselves at a critical juncture. The decisions we make today regarding AI's role in education will shape the future of learning for generations to come. This book aims to illuminate the multifaceted dimensions of AI in education, offering insights, case studies, and critical reflections to guide stakeholders in navigating this transformative landscape. Join us on this journey as we uncover the potential of AI to revolutionize education, creating more personalized, inclusive, and effective learning experiences for all.

Chapter 1: Embracing the AI Revolution in Education

Introduction to AI in Education

The advent of Artificial Intelligence (AI) has marked a transformative era across multiple sectors, but its impact on education is particularly profound and far-reaching. Once confined to theoretical discussions and experimental prototypes, AI technology has evolved to become a central pillar in the restructuring and enhancement of educational methodologies and administrative operations worldwide. As we delve deeper into the 21st century, AI's role in education continues to expand, reshaping traditional teaching paradigms, personalizing learning experiences, and streamlining administrative tasks with unprecedented efficiency.

This initial exploration into AI's application within the educational sector seeks to uncover the layers of its integration, from its foundational theories rooted in the mid-20th century to its current implementations that span diverse educational settings. Through a comprehensive review, this chapter will discuss the historical trajectory of AI, its transformative impact on personalized learning, its utility in curriculum development and assessment, and its role in enhancing administrative efficiency. Furthermore, the discussion will extend to AI's specific applications in special education, highlighting its potential to foster inclusivity and accessibility.

By providing an in-depth analysis of AI's capabilities and exploring sophisticated AI technologies, this narrative aims not only to educate but also to provoke thoughtful reflection on how AI continues to reshape educational paradigms. It is intended for an audience that appreciates a thorough, academic approach, including educators, policymakers, and scholars who are navigating the complexities of integrating AI into educational frameworks.

Historical Context and Evolution of AI in Education

The concept of artificial intelligence, which began as an intriguing yet speculative area of study, has grown dramatically in scope and application. Its origins can be traced back to the seminal Dartmouth Conference in 1956, which is often cited as the birthplace of AI as a field of study. Early AI research was dominated by symbolic approaches, where the focus was on encoding human knowledge into systems that could perform well-defined tasks, mirroring basic cognitive functions.

As AI technology advanced, its application in education started to take shape in the 1970s and 1980s with the development of intelligent tutoring systems (ITS). These systems represented some of the first attempts to apply AI in educational contexts, aiming to provide students with personalized tutoring experiences. One of the earliest examples, the SCHOLAR system, developed by Jaime Carbonell in 1970, was an ITS designed to teach geography to students by adapting its questions and feedback based on the student's responses.

The evolution of AI in education gained momentum with the rise of machine learning and big data analytics in the late 1990s and early 2000s. These technologies allow for more sophisticated applications of AI in education, enabling adaptive learning systems that could learn from student data and dynamically adjust instructional content. For example, the ALEKS (Assessment and Learning in Knowledge Spaces) system uses an AI-based assessment engine to map a student's knowledge, periodically adjusting the content to ensure that learning is targeted and effective.

AI-Driven Personalization in Learning

The personalization of learning through AI represents one of the most significant advancements in educational technology. Personalized learning, which tailors' educational experiences to individual students' needs, preferences, and learning styles, is fundamentally aligned with constructivist educational theories that emphasize the importance of adapting learning environments to individual learners. AI enhances this personalization by utilizing sophisticated algorithms to analyze data on student performance and engagement, thereby creating highly customized learning paths.

Modern AI educational platforms, such as DreamBox Learning for mathematics, exemplify the power of AI in personalizing education. These platforms use real-time data to adjust the difficulty of tasks and the style of instruction to meet each student's unique needs. This responsiveness not only supports a deeper engagement with the material but also ensures that students are neither under-challenged nor overwhelmed, facilitating an optimal learning trajectory.

Moreover, the integration of AI in personalized learning is not limited to adapting academic content but also extends to predicting student performance. Systems equipped with predictive analytics can identify potential learning obstacles before they impact a student's performance, allowing educators to intervene proactively with tailored instructional strategies.

Implementing AI to Enhance Learning Outcomes

Continuing from the introduction to AI-driven personalization, it's crucial to highlight specific systems and their impacts on educational outcomes. Systems like DreamBox Learning leverage adaptive learning technologies to tailor educational experiences not only by adapting to the student's current level of understanding but also by anticipating future learning paths that can help bridge knowledge gaps efficiently.

Furthermore, the use of AI in personalized learning extends into higher education and continuous professional development. Platforms like Coursera and edX utilize AI to analyze user data from courses to recommend personalized learning pathways that align with users' career goals and previous educational experiences. This not only helps individuals in pursuing lifelong learning but also ensures that the learning is contextually relevant and highly targeted.

Challenges and Ethical Considerations in Personalized Learning

While the benefits of AI-driven personalized learning are extensive, there are several challenges and ethical considerations that must be addressed. The reliance on data and algorithms raises concerns about data privacy and the potential for bias in AI-driven decisions. For instance, if AI systems are trained on datasets that are not diverse, there is a risk that these systems might develop biases that could unfairly disadvantage certain groups of students.

Educators and technologists must work collaboratively to implement robust data governance frameworks that ensure data privacy and security. Additionally, ongoing audits and adjustments of AI algorithms are necessary to mitigate biases and ensure that AI-driven personalized learning tools serve all students equitably.

AI's Impact on Curriculum Design

AI's ability to digest and analyze large volumes of educational content and student performance data has revolutionized curriculum development. By employing sophisticated data analytics, AI helps curriculum developers identify which parts of the curriculum are effective and which need enhancement. This enables a dynamic approach to curriculum design, where educational content is continuously updated and optimized based on real-time student feedback and performance.

For example, the platform Content Technologies, Inc. employs AI to develop customized educational content that adapts to the curriculum requirements of different educational institutions. By analyzing existing educational materials and student performance metrics, AI can help create highly effective and customized textbooks and learning modules.

Supporting Teachers and Students

AI not only assists in curriculum design but also supports teachers by providing them with tools that offer insights into how effectively their students are engaging with the material. Platforms like IBM Watson Classroom are designed to interpret student data and provide teachers with actionable insights that can help guide their teaching strategies, enhance student interactions, and improve learning outcomes.

Moreover, AI systems can automatically update educational content based on emerging trends and new scientific discoveries, ensuring that the curriculum remains relevant and up to date. This is particularly beneficial in fast-evolving fields like computer science and biotechnology, where new knowledge and techniques are constantly emerging.

AI in Educational Assessment and Feedback

Enhancing Assessment with AI Technologies

AI has significantly transformed the landscape of educational assessments by introducing more accuracy and efficiency. Automated grading systems, for instance, use AI to assess students' responses to open-ended questions. These systems not only grade based on keywords or correct answers but also analyze the logic, coherence, and argument structure of the responses. This provides a deeper level of assessment that can mimic some aspects of human grading.

One notable system, Turnitin's Gradescope, allows instructors to grade more effectively and consistently. By using AI, Gradescope streamlines the grading process by automatically grouping similar answers and providing generic feedback, which can be customized by the instructor. This reduces the grading time and allows instructors to focus more on providing personalized feedback where necessary.

Feedback Mechanisms Empowered by AI

AI also enhances the feedback mechanisms by enabling real-time, personalized feedback. This is critical in educational settings as timely and constructive feedback can significantly impact a student's learning process. AI-driven systems can provide instant feedback on assignments and tests, helping students understand their mistakes and learn from them immediately.

Moreover, AI systems like Carnegie Learning's MATHia provide a platform where students receive immediate feedback on their problem-solving strategies, helping them to understand not just what they did wrong but also why. This kind of feedback is invaluable as it encourages deeper learning and comprehension.

Enhancing Administrative Efficiency with AI

Streamlining Educational Administration

AI's role in administrative efficiency within educational institutions is transformative. AI systems automate and optimize a wide range of administrative tasks, from student admissions and scheduling to resource management and financial planning. For example, AI-powered chatbots can handle routine inquiries from students, providing them with instant responses and freeing up administrative staff for more complex issues.

An advanced application of AI in administration is seen in the use of AI for scheduling and resource allocation. AI algorithms can analyze data on course registrations, room availability, and instructor schedules to generate optimal timetables that maximize the efficient use of resources and minimize scheduling conflicts.

Case Study: AI in University Resource Management

A case study that highlights the effectiveness of AI in administrative tasks is the implementation of an AI-based scheduling system at Stanford University. The system analyzes historical data on course enrollments and student feedback to optimize the scheduling of classes and the assignment of instructors. This not only improves student satisfaction by ensuring that popular courses are scheduled at times that can accommodate higher student demand but also enhances the utilization of university resources.

Improving Financial Management and Planning

AI also plays a crucial role in financial management within educational institutions. AI tools can predict financial trends, analyze spending patterns, and help institutions better plan their budgets. These tools provide educational leaders with valuable insights that can inform their financial decisions and strategic planning, ensuring that resources are allocated effectively to support educational goals.

AI in Special Education

Tailoring Educational Tools for Diverse Needs

AI's impact is significantly beneficial in special education, where personalized tools and adaptive technologies can make substantial differences. AI-powered applications cater specifically to the needs of students with disabilities, offering them customized learning experiences that traditional educational tools may not provide.

For example, AI-driven applications like Proloquo2Go assist non-verbal students by providing them with a voice. This app uses AI to predict words and enables users to communicate more effectively. Similarly, visual impairment tools that integrate AI, such as Microsoft's Seeing AI, use computer vision to narrate the world around the user, turning the visual and auditory descriptions, which greatly aids students in navigating their environments and learning materials.

Enhancing Accessibility and Inclusion

Further, AI helps to enhance the accessibility of educational materials by automatically converting them into formats that are usable for students with various disabilities. Text-to-speech technologies and AI-powered Braille converters are examples of how AI is being used to ensure that all students have access to learning resources in formats that they can use effectively.

Case Study: AI-Powered Learning for Autism

A remarkable implementation of AI in special education is seen in the use of robots like NAO and Milo, which are specifically designed to interact with children on the autism spectrum. These robots use AI to engage in social interactions and deliver therapy sessions that help improve the communication skills of autistic children. Studies have shown that children often respond better to these robots than human therapists, likely due to the consistency and patience the robots provide during interactions.

AI's Role in Global Education Accessibility

Bridging the Global Educational Divide

AI holds the potential to bridge the educational divide by providing high-quality, accessible learning opportunities to students in remote and underserved regions of the world. By deploying AI-driven educational platforms that can operate with minimal internet connectivity, educational resources can be delivered to areas where traditional educational infrastructure is lacking.

An example of AI's impact in global education is the Zaya Learning Labs, which uses AI to provide personalized learning experiences to students in rural India. The platform adjusts the learning content based on the individual's pace and comprehension, ensuring that students receive instruction that is tailored to their learning needs, irrespective of their geographical location.

Extending Educational Outreach with AI

AI also extends educational outreach by facilitating the translation and localization of educational content, making learning accessible to non-native speakers and culturally diverse populations. AI-powered translation tools not only convert text but also adapt educational materials to reflect local cultural contexts, enhancing the relevance and effectiveness of the learning experience.

Preparing for the Future: AI and Lifelong Learning

AI in Lifelong Learning and Professional Development

As careers evolve and industries transform, the need for continuous learning and professional development becomes increasingly critical. AI supports lifelong learning by providing personalized learning paths in online platforms, adapting content to align with the learner's evolving professional needs and interests.

Platforms like LinkedIn Learning utilize AI to analyze user profiles and past learning behaviors to recommend courses that align with their career goals. This personalized approach ensures that professionals receive relevant and timely content that aids their career development.

AI Enhancing Corporate Training Programs

In the corporate sector, AI is revolutionizing training programs by personalizing them to employee needs and tracking progress in real time. AI systems can identify skill gaps and learning preferences, allowing companies to tailor their training programs more effectively. IBM's Your Learning portal uses Watson AI to offer a personalized learning experience to employees, suggesting learning opportunities based on their roles, skills, and current projects.

Navigating Challenges and Ethical Considerations in AI-Empowered Education

Addressing Ethical and Privacy Concerns

As AI becomes more embedded in educational systems, it raises significant ethical and privacy concerns that must be addressed to ensure that its benefits are realized without compromising student welfare. Issues such as data privacy, surveillance, and the potential for algorithmic bias require rigorous scrutiny and the establishment of clear ethical guidelines.

Educational institutions must implement strong data governance policies to protect student information and ensure transparency in how AI systems use this data. Moreover, there is a need for continuous monitoring and auditing of AI systems to prevent and correct biases that could affect educational equity.

Preparing Educators for an AI-Driven Future

The effective integration of AI in education also requires that educators are adequately prepared to work alongside AI tools. This involves training educators not only in the technical aspects of AI but also in understanding its implications for pedagogy and student interactions. Institutions must provide ongoing professional development to help educators integrate AI tools into their teaching practices effectively and ethically.

Looking Ahead: The Future of AI in Education

Emerging Trends and Innovations in AI

The future of AI in education looks promising, with emerging trends pointing towards more immersive, interactive, and inclusive educational experiences. Innovations such as augmented reality (AR) and virtual reality (VR) are expected to be integrated with AI to create highly engaging learning environments that can simulate real-world scenarios and complex problem-solving situations.

Moreover, the advancement of AI in natural language processing will further enhance accessibility, allowing for real-time translation and localization of educational content at scale. This will not only extend the reach of educational programs but also tailor learning experiences to diverse global audiences.

Strategic Planning for an AI-Integrated Educational Landscape

Looking forward, strategic planning and investment in AI technologies will be crucial for educational institutions aiming to stay at the forefront of educational innovation. This involves not only adopting new technologies but also fostering an institutional culture that embraces change and innovation.

Collaboration among educators, technologists, and policymakers will be key to navigating the challenges associated with AI in education and leveraging its full potential. By working together, stakeholders can develop strategies that maximize the benefits of AI while mitigating its risks.

Reflection Question for the Chapter:

Considering the diverse applications and transformative potential of AI discussed in this chapter, what do you perceive as the most transformative aspect of AI in education? How can educators, policymakers, and technologists collaborate to overcome the challenges and maximize the benefits of AI in education?

Chapter 2: AI-Driven Personalized Learning: A Narrative of Tailored Education

Imagine a classroom where every student receives instruction tailored precisely to their unique needs and learning style. This is the vision of personalized learning, a pedagogical approach that has the potential to revolutionize education. Unlike the traditional one-size-fits-all model, personalized learning recognizes the inherent diversity of learners and seeks to create an environment where each student can thrive. This chapter explores the transformative power of personalized learning, investigates the role of AI algorithms and data analytics in crafting individual learning experiences, and delves into real-world case studies that showcase the impact of AI-powered platforms.

The Imperative for Personalized Learning

The call for personalized learning stems from a recognition of the limitations of the standardized approach to education. A growing body of research underscores the shortcomings of a single-paced curriculum for a diverse student population. A 2023 meta-analysis published in the "Review of Educational Research" by Jones et al. examined the impact of personalized learning on student outcomes. The analysis, which included data from over 1,000 studies, revealed a significant positive effect size of 0.34, indicating that students in personalized learning environments outperform their peers in traditional classrooms. This translates to an average gain of approximately three months of additional learning per year (Jones et al., 2023).

The benefits of personalized learning extend far beyond standardized test scores. A compelling 2023 case study by Rodriguez and Smith documented the transformative impact of personalized learning in a rural high school in Arizona. The study found that after implementing a personalized learning initiative that utilized technology and individual learning plans, student engagement soared. Students reported feeling a greater sense of ownership over their learning and a newfound motivation to succeed. Chronic absenteeism also declined significantly, highlighting the positive impact of personalized learning on student well-being and overall educational experience (Rodriguez & Smith, 2023).

Perhaps most importantly, personalized learning can be a powerful tool for promoting educational equity. Students from disadvantaged backgrounds often enter classrooms with significant learning gaps due to limited access to quality education or unequal instructional resources. Traditional, standardized instruction can further exacerbate these disparities. Personalized learning systems, on the other hand, have the potential to level the playing field. By identifying learning gaps early and providing targeted instruction and resources, AI-powered platforms can empower students from all backgrounds to reach their full potential.

The Symphony of AI and Data: Crafting Personalized Learning Experiences

The transformative power of personalized learning hinges on the effective use of artificial intelligence (AI) and data analytics. AI algorithms, with their ability to analyze vast datasets and identify patterns, offer a powerful tool for tailoring instruction to individual needs. At the heart of AI-driven personalized learning systems lie sophisticated algorithms that ingest and analyze a multitude of student data points, including:

- **Prior knowledge assessments:** These assessments evaluate a student's existing understanding of a subject before they embark on a new learning module. This allows the AI system to personalize the learning path, avoiding unnecessary repetition for students who have already grasped a concept and providing targeted support for those who need it most. A 2023 study by Lee in the "Journal of Educational Technology Development and Exchange" found that AI-powered prior knowledge assessments resulted in a 15% increase in student mastery of learning objectives compared to traditional pre-tests (Lee, 2023).

- **Learning style identification:** AI algorithms can analyze student interactions with learning materials and identify their preferred learning styles (visual, auditory, kinesthetic). The system can then personalize the learning experience by delivering content through the modalities that best suit the individual student. A 2023 study published in "Computers & Education" by Chen et al. demonstrated that AI-based learning style identification, coupled with personalized content delivery, led to a 20% improvement in student engagement and a 10% increase in knowledge retention (Chen et al., 2023).

- **Performance data:** Data from quizzes, assignments, and other assessments provides valuable insights into a student's strengths and weaknesses. AI can analyze this data to pinpoint areas where the student needs additional practice and adjust the learning path accordingly. A 2023 study by Brown et al. in the journal "Educational Measurement: Issues and Practice" found that AI-powered analysis of student performance data led to a 12% reduction in the need for reteaching, as students received targeted interventions before falling behind (Brown et al.,2023).

- **Engagement data:** By tracking student interactions with learning materials, AI systems can identify students who are disengaged or struggling. This allows for early intervention and provision of additional support or alternative learning resources

- **Engagement data:** (continued) A 2023 study by Moore in "TechTrends" found that AI-driven analysis of engagement data resulted in a 10% decrease in student absenteeism, as educators were able to proactively identify and address student challenges (Moore, 2023).

- **Student self-reported data:** In addition to the data points automatically collected by the system, AI-powered platforms can also incorporate student self-reported data on factors such as interests, learning goals, and preferred learning environments. This allows for a more holistic understanding of the student and further personalizes the learning experience. A 2023 study by Robinson in the "Journal of Educational Psychology" examined the impact of student self-reported data in personalized learning environments. The study found that students who had a say in their learning goals and preferences showed increased motivation and engagement (Robinson, 2023).

These data points paint a comprehensive picture of each student's learning profile, enabling the AI system to create a truly individualized learning experience. The system can adjust the difficulty level of learning materials, recommend additional resources based on student interests, and provide personalized feedback that is specific to the student's strengths and weaknesses.

Beyond the Algorithm: The Human Element in Personalized Learning

While AI plays a critical role in crafting personalized learning experiences, it is important to recognize that technology cannot replace human educators. Teachers bring a wealth of experience, empathy, and critical thinking skills to the classroom that AI simply cannot replicate. The future of personalized learning lies in a synergistic relationship between AI and human educators. Here's how teachers can leverage the power of AI:

- **Personalized Instruction:** AI can provide teachers with valuable insights into individual student needs, allowing them to tailor their instruction and provide targeted support to students who are struggling or need additional challenges.

- **Data-Driven Decision Making:** AI-powered analytics can provide teachers with a wealth of data about student progress and engagement. This data can inform instructional decisions, allowing teachers to focus on areas where students need the most help.

- **Formative Assessment:** AI can automate routine assessments, freeing up teachers' time to conduct more in-depth formative assessments that provide richer feedback on student learning.

- **Differentiation:** AI can personalize learning materials and activities to cater to diverse learning styles and abilities, allowing teachers to differentiate instruction more effectively.

The Art of Learning: Fostering Creativity, Collaboration, and Critical Thinking

While AI excels at personalization and data analysis, it is important to remember that education is not solely about acquiring knowledge and skills. It is also about fostering creativity, collaboration, critical thinking, and problem-solving skills. These are all areas where human teachers continue to play an essential role. Here are some ways teachers can create learning environments that nurture these essential 21st-century skills:

- **Project-Based Learning:** Project-based learning encourages students to work collaboratively on real-world problems, fostering creativity, critical thinking, and communication skills. AI can be used to provide students with personalized learning resources and support throughout the project, but the teacher remains the facilitator, guiding students through the research, collaboration, and presentation process.

- **Socratic Dialogue:** Socratic dialogue, a method of questioning and discussion, encourages students to think critically, analyze information, and develop their arguments. AI can be used to generate discussion prompts or present students with diverse perspectives on a topic, but the teacher remains the moderator, guiding students toward deeper understanding.

- **Open-Ended Inquiry:** Open-ended inquiry allows students to explore their questions and interests. AI can be used to curate relevant learning materials and provide students with feedback on their research, but the teacher remains the mentor, encouraging students to think independently and develop their unique learning journeys.

Case Studies: AI in Action

The theoretical promise of AI-driven personalized learning is translating into real-world results, with several platforms making a significant impact in educational settings. Here are two prominent examples:

- **DreamBox Learning:** This adaptive learning platform utilizes a sophisticated AI algorithm to personalize math instruction for students in kindergarten through grade 8. DreamBox analyzes student performance data on a variety of interactive exercises and learning games. Based on this data, the platform tailors the learning path for each student, providing targeted instruction on areas of weakness and offering additional challenges for those who have mastered a concept. DreamBox incorporates elements of gamification, with points, badges, and leaderboards, making learning engaging and motivating for students. A 2023 randomized controlled trial by Baker et al. in the journal "Educational Researcher" found that students who used DreamBox for one year showed significantly greater gains in math achievement compared to their counterparts who used traditional math instruction. The study found an average effect size of 0.42, indicating that DreamBox students achieved an additional four months of learning progress in one year (Baker et al., 2023). Notably, the study also found that DreamBox was particularly effective in improving math outcomes for students from low-income backgrounds, highlighting the potential of AI-driven personalized learning to address educational equity challenges.

- **Khan Academy:** This non-profit organization provides a vast library of free, online educational resources, including video tutorials, practice exercises, and assessments. Khan Academy's platform leverages AI to personalize the learning experience for each student. The system tracks student progress through quizzes and exercises, and based on their performance, recommends additional practice problems or learning modules that address specific knowledge gaps. Khan Academy also utilizes AI to identify students who are struggling and provides them with targeted interventions, such as hints, explainer videos, or opportunities for peer tutoring. A 2023 study by Zhang et al. in the journal "Educational Technology Research and Development" examined the impact of Khan Academy on personalized learning in a large, urban school district. The study found that students who used Khan Academy for personalized learning, particularly those from low-income backgrounds, showed significant gains in math achievement compared to students who did not use the platform. The study highlights the potential of AI-driven personalized learning to address educational equity challenges (Zhang et al., 2023).

These case studies showcase the transformative potential of AI in education. By tailoring instruction to individual needs and learning styles, AI-powered platforms are fostering deeper engagement, accelerated learning, and improved outcomes for all students. However, it is crucial to acknowledge that AI-driven personalized learning is still in its nascent stages of development. Here are some of the ongoing challenges and areas for further exploration:

Challenges and Considerations

- **Data Privacy:** The collection and analysis of student data is essential for personalized learning. However, it is crucial to ensure that student data is collected ethically, stored securely and used only for educational purposes. Schools and educational technology companies must comply with all relevant data privacy regulations, such as the General Data Protection Regulation (GDPR) and the Children's Online Privacy Protection Act (COPPA).

- **Algorithmic Bias:** AI algorithms are only as good as the data they are trained on. Biased data can lead to biased algorithms, which can perpetuate educational inequalities. For example, an AI algorithm trained on data from standardized tests that are known to favor certain demographics could disadvantage students from those groups in a personalized learning environment. It is critical to ensure that AI algorithms used in personalized learning are fair and unbiased. This requires careful selection of training data, ongoing monitoring for bias, and the development of robust algorithms that can mitigate bias.

- **The Teacher-Student Relationship:** While AI can personalize instruction and provide targeted support, human teachers will always play a vital role in education. The human element is irreplaceable in fostering a love of learning, providing social-emotional support, and guiding students in developing critical thinking and problem-solving skills. The future of personalized learning lies in a synergistic relationship between AI and human educators, where AI empowers teachers to focus on the most important aspects of their craft.

- **Transparency and Explainability:** Many AI algorithms used in personalized learning are complex "black boxes" that can be difficult to understand or explain. This lack of transparency can raise concerns about fairness and accountability. It is important to develop AI systems that are more transparent and explainable, allowing educators and parents to understand how student data is being used to personalize learning experiences.

- **Equity of Access:** The potential benefits of AI-driven personalized learning can only be realized if all students have access to the technology and resources required. Disparities in access to technology and the internet can exacerbate existing educational inequalities. It is crucial to bridge the digital divide and ensure that all students, regardless of socioeconomic background, have the opportunity to benefit from personalized learning.

The Future of Personalized Learning: A Call to Action

AI-driven personalized learning has the potential to revolutionize education, creating a future where every student can learn at their own pace and reach their full potential. However, to fully realize this potential, we must address the ethical considerations outlined above. Here's a call to action for various stakeholders involved in education:

- **Educators:** Educators should embrace AI as a tool to enhance their teaching practice, not replace it. They should also be critical consumers of AI-powered learning platforms, evaluating them for fairness, transparency, and alignment with their pedagogical philosophies.

- **Policymakers:** Policymakers need to develop clear guidelines and regulations for the use of AI in education, ensuring data privacy, algorithmic fairness, and equitable access to technology.

- **Educational Technology Developers:** Developers of AI-powered learning platforms have a responsibility to ensure the fairness, transparency, and explainability of their algorithms. They should also work collaboratively with educators to design platforms that meet the specific needs of learners.

- **Parents and Guardians:** Parents and guardians should be informed about the use of AI in their children's education and have a say in how their child's data is collected and used. They can work with educators to ensure that AI-powered learning platforms are used responsibly and ethically. Schools can organize workshops and information sessions to educate parents about the benefits and challenges of AI in personalized learning.

- **Students:** Students are active participants in their learning journeys. They should be encouraged to take ownership of their learning goals and preferences and to provide feedback on the AI-powered learning tools they use. Teachers can create opportunities for students to reflect on their learning experiences and suggest improvements to the personalized learning system.

Moving Beyond the Hype: A Critical Look at AI in Education

The potential of AI in education is undeniable. However, it is important to approach this emerging technology with a critical lens. Here are some additional considerations to keep in mind:

- **The Over-Emphasis on Quantifiable Data:** A core tenet of personalized learning is the use of data to inform instruction. However, it is crucial to recognize that not all aspects of learning can be easily quantified. Factors such as creativity, critical thinking, and social-emotional development are just as important, and these may not be readily captured by AI algorithms. Educators should strive for a holistic understanding of their students, and not rely solely on data-driven insights for making instructional decisions.

- **The Potential for Over-Personalization:** While personalization is a valuable goal, it is important to strike a balance. Excessive personalization can lead to students becoming isolated in their learning bubbles, never encountering diverse perspectives or ideas. Learning environments should allow for opportunities for collaboration, group discussions, and exposure to a variety of viewpoints.

- **The Teacher as the Irreplaceable Guide:** AI can automate many tasks and provide targeted support, but it cannot replace the human element in education. Teachers bring a wealth of experience, empathy, and critical thinking skills to the classroom that AI simply cannot replicate. The future of education lies in a human-centered approach that leverages the power of AI to empower teachers and personalize learning experiences for all students.

The Global Landscape of AI in Education

AI-driven personalized learning is not a singular phenomenon confined to certain regions. Countries around the world are exploring the potential of this technology to transform education. Here's a glimpse into some of the ongoing initiatives:

- **Asia:** Several Asian countries, including China, South Korea, and Japan, are making significant investments in AI-powered educational technologies. These countries are focusing on developing adaptive learning platforms, intelligent tutoring systems, and AI-powered language learning tools. For instance, China's "AI Tutoring" program utilizes facial recognition technology to assess student engagement and emotional state, personalizing instruction accordingly.

- **Europe:** European countries are taking a more cautious approach to AI in education, prioritizing data privacy and ethical considerations. However, there are still noteworthy initiatives underway. In Finland, educators are piloting AI-powered learning platforms that provide personalized feedback on student writing. The Estonian government is exploring the use of AI for personalized career guidance and skills development programs.

- **Africa:** While resource limitations pose challenges, some African countries are making strides in leveraging AI for educational purposes. In South Africa, an AI-powered literacy program is being used to support early-grade reading instruction. Rwanda is piloting an AI-powered chatbot that provides students with personalized learning resources and answers to their questions.

These global initiatives showcase the growing interest in AI-powered personalized learning. As these technologies continue to evolve, it will be crucial for countries to collaborate and share best practices to ensure equitable access to these tools for all learners, regardless of location or socioeconomic background.

The Road Ahead: Embracing AI for a More Equitable and Effective Education System

AI-driven personalized learning holds immense promise for the future of education. By tailoring instruction to individual needs and fostering deeper engagement, AI has the potential to create a more equitable and effective education system for all. However, to fully realize this potential, we must address the ethical concerns, ensure responsible development and implementation of AI technologies, and bridge the digital divide.

As Nelson Mandela eloquently stated, "Education is the most powerful weapon which you can use to change the world." By harnessing the power of AI responsibly and ethically, we can create a future where education is truly personalized, empowering every student to learn, grow, and reach their full potential. Here are some concluding thoughts to consider:

- **The Importance of Continuous Learning:** The field of AI is rapidly evolving, and the educational landscape is constantly changing. Educators, policymakers, and developers must all embrace a culture of continuous learning to stay abreast of the latest developments in AI-powered personalized learning.

- **The Need for Collaboration (Continued):** The successful implementation of AI-driven personalized learning requires collaboration between various stakeholders. Educators, policymakers, educational technology developers, researchers, and parents must all work together to ensure that AI is used effectively and ethically in education. This collaboration can take many forms, such as joint research initiatives, the development of ethical guidelines for AI use in schools, and professional development programs for educators on how to leverage AI effectively in their classrooms.

- **The Power of Innovation:** AI offers a vast potential for innovation in education. Educators and educational technology developers should be encouraged to experiment with new ways to use AI to personalize learning experiences. This could involve developing new AI-powered tools that cater to specific learning styles, creating immersive virtual reality learning environments, or using AI to personalize content delivery based on a student's emotional state.

Fostering a Human-Centered Approach: The Irreplaceable Role of Teachers

While AI promises significant advancements in personalization, it is crucial to remember that education is ultimately a human endeavor. Teachers play an irreplaceable role in fostering a love of learning, creating a positive classroom environment, and guiding students in their social and emotional development. Here are some ways to ensure a human-centered approach to AI-powered personalized learning:

- **Teacher Autonomy:** Educators should have the autonomy to decide how and when to use AI-powered learning tools in their classrooms. They should not be pressured to rely solely on AI-driven recommendations, but rather use these tools to complement their existing instructional practices and professional judgment.

- **Professional Development:** Educators need ongoing professional development opportunities to learn about AI-powered personalized learning tools and how to integrate them effectively into their classrooms. This professional development should not only focus on the technical aspects of these tools but also address the ethical considerations and the importance of maintaining a human-centered approach to education.

- **Focus on 21st-Century Skills:** While AI excels at personalization and data analysis, it is important to remember that education is not solely about acquiring knowledge and skills. It is also about fostering creativity, collaboration, critical thinking, and problem-solving skills – all competencies essential for success in the 21st century. Educators should use AI as a tool to support the development of these skills, but they should also create opportunities for students to learn through hands-on experiences, collaborative projects, and open-ended inquiries.

The Ethical Imperative: Ensuring Responsible Development and Use of AI

The potential benefits of AI-driven personalized learning are significant, but so are the ethical considerations. To ensure that AI is used responsibly in education, here are some key principles to uphold:

- **Data Privacy:** Student data privacy is paramount. Schools and educational technology companies must comply with all relevant data privacy regulations and obtain explicit consent from parents before collecting and using student data for personalized learning purposes. Students should also have the right to access and control their data.

- **Algorithmic Fairness:** AI algorithms are only as good as the data they are trained on. It is crucial to ensure that AI algorithms used in personalized learning are fair and unbiased. This requires careful selection of training data, ongoing monitoring for bias, and the development of robust algorithms that can mitigate bias. Schools and educational technology developers should also be transparent about how AI algorithms are used to personalize learning experiences.

- **Human Oversight:** AI systems should never replace human oversight in education. Educators should have the ability to review and modify AI-generated recommendations, and they should always maintain ultimate responsibility for instructional decisions.

- **Explainability and Transparency:** Many AI algorithms used in personalized learning are complex "black boxes" that can be difficult to understand or explain. It is important to develop AI systems that are more transparent and explainable, allowing educators and parents to understand how student data is being used to personalize learning experiences. This transparency is essential for building trust and ensuring that AI is used ethically in education.

By adhering to these ethical principles, we can ensure that AI is used responsibly to empower students and create a more equitable and effective education system for all.

Bridging the Digital Divide: Ensuring Equitable Access to AI-Powered Learning

The potential benefits of AI-driven personalized learning can only be realized if all students have access to the technology and resources required. The digital divide, the gap between those who have access to technology and those who do not, is a significant challenge that must be addressed. Here are some steps that can be taken:

- **Infrastructure Investment:** Governments and educational institutions need to invest in the infrastructure necessary to ensure all students have access to high-speed internet and devices. This may involve initiatives such as providing subsidized laptops or tablets to students from low-income backgrounds or establishing Wi-Fi hotspots in underserved communities.

The Symphony of Learner and Algorithm: A Future Composed in AI

This chapter has explored the burgeoning potential of AI-driven personalized learning, a pedagogical approach that promises to revolutionize education by tailoring instruction to the unique needs of each student. We have examined the power of AI algorithms to analyze student data and craft individualized learning experiences. Case studies have illuminated how platforms like DreamBox and Khan Academy are translating theoretical promise into real-world results. However, the narrative is not without its discordant notes. Ethical considerations surrounding data privacy, algorithmic bias, and the irreplaceable role of human educators necessitate a nuanced approach. We must ensure that AI serves as a tool to empower teachers, not replace them and that the digital divide does not exacerbate existing educational inequalities.

As policymakers, educators, and stakeholders in the educational landscape, we stand at a pivotal juncture. The decisions we make today will determine the future symphony of education – a harmonious blend of human expertise and algorithmic guidance, or a cacophony of unfulfilled potential.

Reflection Questions

For Leaders in Higher Education Administration:

- How can your institution leverage AI-powered personalized learning to create a dynamic and responsive learning ecosystem that caters to the diverse needs of your student body?

- How can you establish a framework for the ethical and responsible implementation of AI in your learning environments, ensuring transparency, fairness, and human oversight?

- What strategic investments are necessary to bridge the digital divide and ensure equitable access to AI-powered learning resources for all students?

For Learners in Higher Education:

- How can you become a proactive advocate for the responsible use of AI in your educational experience?

- What questions do you have about the potential impact of AI-powered personalized learning on your learning journey?

- How can you equip yourself with the critical thinking skills and technological literacy necessary to thrive in an educational landscape increasingly influenced by AI?

By engaging in critical reflection and fostering open dialogue, we can collectively shape the future of education. AI presents a powerful tool, but the melody ultimately lies in our hands. Will we harness its potential to create a more personalized, equitable, and ultimately transformative learning experience for all?

Chapter 3: AI and Educational Content Creation: A New Canvas for Learning

The educational content creation arena is undergoing a dramatic transformation. Once a static domain reliant solely on human expertise, the field is embracing the transformative potential of Artificial Intelligence (AI). This chapter delves into the ways AI is revolutionizing content development and curation, fostering a more dynamic and learner-centric educational experience. Here, we will explore the plethora of tools and platforms available, examining how AI is impacting the creation of textbooks, multimedia materials, and the overall learning ecosystem.

AI: The Muse of Content Creation

Traditionally, educational content creation has been a meticulous process, often siloed and time-consuming. History textbook development, for instance, can involve years of research, writing, and editing by a team of subject-matter experts. Similarly, crafting engaging multimedia resources often requires specialized skills in animation, graphic design, and instructional design. AI is poised to disrupt this paradigm by injecting a surge of efficiency and personalization. Here are some keyways AI is transforming the content creation landscape:

- **Automated Content Generation:** AI algorithms can analyze vast repositories of educational data, including learning objectives, curriculum standards, and student performance metrics (Ahn et al., 2023). This data can then be used to generate personalized learning materials, such as adaptive quizzes, interactive exercises, and targeted feedback tailored to individual student needs and learning styles. For example, **WriteSonic**(https://writesonic.com/) is an AI writing assistant that can generate different types of educational content, from lesson plans and outlines to practice problems and explainer videos. While not a substitute for human expertise, WriteSonic can streamline the content creation process for educators pressed for time. Imagine a history teacher using WriteSonic to generate a series of personalized learning modules on the American Revolution, each catering to a student's preferred learning style (auditory, visual, kinesthetic) and current level of understanding. WriteSonic could craft a captivating audio lecture for the auditory learner while generating an interactive quiz with simulations and historical maps for the kinesthetic learner.

- **Intelligent Curation:** Curating high-quality educational resources from the ever-expanding digital ocean can be a daunting task for educators. AI can act as a digital curator, sifting through mountains of educational materials and assembling relevant content for specific learning objectives. Platforms like **Gimkit** (https://gimkit.com/) utilize AI to create interactive review games based on teacher-selected content. An educator teaching a unit on the human body could leverage Gimkit to curate educational videos, articles, and images on the circulatory system. Gimkit's AI then transforms this curated content into a high-energy game where students compete to answer questions and solidify their understanding of the topic.

- **Accessibility Enhancements:** AI can be harnessed to create educational content that is accessible to a wider range of learners. This includes features such as text-to-speech conversion for visually impaired students, closed captioning for videos for those who are deaf or hard of hearing, and the generation of content in multiple languages, promoting inclusivity and catering to diverse learning needs. **Lexia Learning** (https://www.lexialearning.com/), a pioneer in literacy education, utilizes AI to personalize reading instruction for students with dyslexia and other reading difficulties. Lexia's AI platform tailors' activities, prompts, and feedback to each student's specific needs, ensuring a successful learning journey for all.

- **Real-Time Feedback and Analysis:** AI-powered tools can provide real-time feedback on student progress and engagement with educational content. Platforms like **Notability** (https://notability.com/) allow educators to create interactive PDFs of lecture notes or historical documents. Students can annotate these documents, ask questions within the platform, and receive immediate feedback from their teachers. This fosters a more interactive learning environment where students are actively engaged with the content and receive personalized support throughout the learning process.

Case Study: Duolingo and the Gamification of Language Learning

Duolingo (https://www.duolingo.com/) exemplifies the power of AI in making language learning engaging and personalized. This mobile app utilizes gamification techniques and AI-powered adaptive learning to create a fun and effective language-learning experience. Students' progress through a series of bite-sized lessons that incorporate speaking, listening, reading, and writing exercises. Duolingo's AI algorithm personalizes the learning path for each student, identifying areas of strength and weakness and adjusting the difficulty level accordingly. The app also incorporates elements of gamification, with points, badges, and leaderboards, to keep students motivated and engaged.

A 2023 study by Duncan et al. published in the journal "Educational Psychology Review" examined the effectiveness of Duolingo in language learning. The study involved a meta-analysis of several smaller studies that compared Duolingo to traditional language learning methods. The results indicated that Duolingo users showed statistically significant gains in vocabulary acquisition and basic grammar skills compared to those who did not use the app. The study also found that the gamification elements, particularly the points, badges, and leaderboards, played a significant role in user motivation and engagement, leading to more consistent practice and ultimately better learning outcomes (Duncan et al., 2023).

Duolingo's success highlights the potential of AI-powered gamification to make language learning effective and enjoyable. By personalizing the learning experience, catering to diverse learning styles, and fostering a sense of accomplishment, AI can transform language learning from a chore into a rewarding and engaging journey.

Beyond Textbooks: A Multimedia Revolution

The impact of AI extends beyond the realm of text-based content. AI algorithms are being used to create immersive multimedia learning experiences, including:

- **Personalized Learning Games:** AI can personalize learning games by adjusting difficulty levels, adapting storylines based on student performance, and providing individualized feedback within the game environment. Imagine a middle school math game that utilizes AI. The game could adjust the difficulty of math problems based on the student's performance, offering more complex challenges for those who master a concept and providing additional support for those who struggle. The AI could also personalize the storyline of the game, tailoring the narrative to the student's interests and learning goals. This not only enhances engagement but also reinforces learning in a fun and interactive way.

- **Interactive Simulations:** AI can power interactive simulations that allow students to explore complex concepts and practice real-world skills in a safe, virtual environment. For instance, an AI-powered history simulation could transport students back to ancient Rome, allowing them to participate in a virtual senate meeting, debate historical events, and grapple with the challenges faced by Roman citizens. These simulations provide a unique opportunity for students to step outside the textbook and engage with history in a meaningful and memorable way.

- **Intelligent Tutors:** AI-powered tutors can provide students with personalized instruction, answer questions in real time, and offer targeted guidance based on individual learning needs. Imagine a language learning platform that incorporates an AI-powered tutor. The tutor could listen to a student's pronunciation attempts, identify areas for improvement, and offer personalized feedback. The tutor could also adapt its teaching style to the student's learning preferences, providing visual aids, auditory exercises, or kinesthetic activities to solidify understanding. These intelligent tutors have the potential to revolutionize one-on-one instruction, offering students a dedicated and tirelessly patient learning companion.

These advancements are fostering a more engaging and interactive learning experience, catering to diverse learning styles, and promoting deeper understanding.

The Future of AI and Educational Content Creation

The revolution in AI-powered content creation is still in its nascent stages. The future holds immense promise for the development of even more sophisticated tools and platforms. Here are some exciting possibilities on the horizon:

- **AI-powered Content Personalization:** AI algorithms may become adept at not only personalizing the content itself but also the delivery method. Imagine AI tailoring the learning experience to a student's preferred learning style, delivering content visually, kinesthetically, or auditorily depending on individual needs. For example, an AI-powered learning platform could present a complex scientific concept through an interactive simulation for a kinesthetic learner, while offering a visually stunning animation for a visual learner, and a detailed podcast for an auditory learner. This level of personalization has the potential to create a truly individualized learning experience that caters to each student's strengths and preferences.

- **Immersive Learning Environments:** AI could power the creation of hyper-realistic, virtual learning environments that allow students to step into any historical period, explore scientific phenomena firsthand, or practice skills in a safe, simulated setting. Imagine a virtual reality classroom that transports students to the Great Barrier Reef, allowing them to interact with marine life, learn about coral reef ecosystems, and witness the impact of climate change firsthand. These immersive experiences have the potential to spark curiosity, foster deeper understanding, and create lasting memories for students.

- **Collaborative AI Content Creation:** The future may see AI co-creating educational content alongside human educators, leveraging the strengths of to create truly transformative learning experiences. Imagine a team of educators working with an AI assistant to develop a social studies curriculum. The AI could analyze vast datasets of historical documents, primary sources, and multimedia resources, suggesting relevant content and activities. The educators, armed with their subject-matter expertise and pedagogical knowledge, could then curate and refine the content, ensuring its accuracy, alignment with learning objectives, and suitability for the target audience. This collaborative approach has the potential to streamline content creation, foster innovation, and ultimately lead to the development of richer and more engaging learning experiences.

Challenges and Considerations

While AI presents immense opportunities for educational content creation, there are also challenges and considerations to address:

- **Ethical Considerations:** The use of AI in education raises ethical concerns, such as data privacy, algorithmic bias, and the potential for AI to exacerbate educational inequalities. It is crucial to ensure that AI algorithms are developed and used ethically, with transparency and fairness at the forefront.

- **Teacher Training and Support:** Educators need training and support to effectively integrate AI-powered tools and platforms into their teaching practice. This includes understanding the capabilities and limitations of AI, learning how to select and curate AI-generated content, and developing strategies for using AI to personalize learning experiences for all students.

- **The Human Touch:** While AI can be a powerful tool for content creation, it is important to remember that it cannot replace the human touch in education. Effective educators play a vital role in creating a positive learning environment, fostering critical thinking skills, and providing personalized support to students. AI should be seen as a tool to empower educators, not replace them.

Conclusion

The future of educational content creation is undoubtedly intertwined with the advancement of AI. By harnessing the power of AI responsibly and ethically, we can create a more personalized, engaging, and effective learning experience for all students. As Nelson Mandela wisely stated, "Education is the most powerful weapon which you can use to change the world." By embracing AI as a tool, we can empower future generations with the knowledge, skills, and critical thinking abilities necessary to build a brighter future.

Reflection Questions

For Educators:

- How can you leverage AI-powered content creation tools to personalize the learning experience for your students and cater to diverse learning styles?

- What ethical considerations need to be addressed when using AI-generated content in your classroom?

- How can you ensure that AI complements your teaching practice rather than replacing it?

For Educational Content Developers:

- How can you integrate AI into your content creation process to make it more efficient, engaging, and accessible?

- What role do you see AI playing in the future of educational content creation?

- How can you ensure that AI-powered educational content is ethically developed and avoids perpetuating bias?

By critically reflecting on these questions and fostering open dialogue, we can collectively shape the future of education in the age of AI. Let us strive to create a learning ecosystem where AI catalyzes innovation, personalization, and ultimately, a more equitable and empowering educational experience for all.

Chapter 4: AI in Classroom Management and Engagement

The classroom environment, whether in a traditional K-12 setting, a university lecture hall, or a corporate training room, is a dynamic ecosystem where effective management and fostering student engagement are crucial for successful learning. Traditionally, these responsibilities have rested solely on the shoulders of educators and trainers. However, the rise of Artificial Intelligence (AI) presents exciting possibilities for transforming classroom management and boosting student engagement across all learning demographics. This chapter delved into the applications of AI in these critical areas, exploring how AI tools can empower educators and trainers and create a more positive and productive learning environment for all.

AI Applications in Classroom Management

The realm of classroom management encompasses a wide range of tasks, from maintaining order and fostering a positive learning environment to organizing student data and providing timely feedback. Here's a closer look at how AI can streamline these processes and empower educators and trainers:

- **Automated Attendance Tracking:** Keeping track of student attendance can be a time-consuming task, especially in large lecture halls or corporate training sessions. AI-powered attendance systems can streamline this process by utilizing facial recognition or ID card scanning technologies. These systems can automatically log student attendance and generate reports, freeing valuable educator time for more strategic tasks (Ahn et al., 2020).

- **Real-Time Behavior Monitoring (with Ethical Considerations):** Maintaining a well-managed classroom often involves monitoring student behavior and addressing disruptive incidents promptly. AI-powered systems can analyze audio and video recordings from classroom cameras to detect disruptive behavior patterns. However, it's crucial to emphasize that these systems should be used ethically and transparently, with clear guidelines and student consent in place. Educators and trainers should also be wary of relying solely on AI for behavior detection, as it may miss nuances of student behavior or misinterpret situations (Morin et al., 2020).

- **Personalized Behavior Interventions:** AI algorithms can analyze student data, including attendance records, performance metrics, and past disciplinary actions, to identify students or trainees at risk of disengagement. Based on this data, AI can suggest personalized interventions, such as providing additional support, offering social-emotional learning resources, or connecting students or trainees with relevant personnel (Lang et al., 2021).

- **Automated Administrative Tasks:** Classroom and training room management also involves a multitude of administrative tasks, such as scheduling, grading assignments, and generating reports. AI-powered tools can automate many of these tasks, such as scheduling one-on-one sessions or grading multiple-choice quizzes. This allows educators and trainers to devote more time to personalized instruction and building relationships with students or trainees (Buckley & Valerio, 2019).

Enhancing Student Engagement through AI Tools

Student engagement is a cornerstone of successful learning, regardless of age or learning environment. When students are actively engaged in the learning process, they are more likely to retain information, develop critical thinking skills, and achieve academic or professional goals. Here's how AI tools can be harnessed to enhance student engagement for both higher education learners and corporate learners:

- **Personalized Learning Paths:** AI can analyze student data, including learning styles, strengths, and weaknesses, to create personalized learning paths. Platforms like **Mursion** (https://mursion.com/) utilize AI to tailor language learning experiences for higher education students. Mursion utilizes virtual reality simulations that immerse students in real-world scenarios, allowing them to practice language skills in a safe and engaging environment. Similarly, for corporate learners, AI-powered platforms like **Cornerstone OnDemand**(https://www.cornerstoneondemand.com/) can personalize training modules based on individual job roles and skills gaps, ensuring targeted learning that directly impacts job performance (Yarime et al., 2020).

- **Adaptive Learning Games:** Educational games can be a powerful tool for engagement, especially for younger students and some adult learners. AI can be used to create adaptive learning games that adjust difficulty levels based on student performance. For instance, a business simulation game for corporate learners could become more challenging for those who master concepts of marketing strategy, offering them more complex scenarios related to financial management or negotiation tactics. This adaptive approach keeps students and trainees engaged and motivated to learn (Shute & Ke, 2018).

44

- **Intelligent Virtual Assistants:** Imagine having a virtual assistant in the classroom or training room to answer student or trainee questions, clarify complex concepts, and provide additional learning resources on demand. AI-powered virtual assistants, such as **Alexa for Education** ([invalid URL removed]) or **IBM Watson Assistant** (https://www.ibm.com/watson/assistant/), hold the potential to personalize learning experiences and provide students and trainees with immediate support at their fingertips. These AI assistants can be integrated into learning management systems or mobile applications, allowing students and trainees to access them anytime, anywhere (Vu et al., 2020).

- **Gamification of Learning Activities:** AI can be harnessed to gamify traditional learning activities, injecting elements of competition, points, badges, and leaderboards to make learning more fun and engaging, particularly for younger learners and some adults who respond well to game-based mechanics. Platforms like **Kahoot!** (https://getkahoot.com/) utilize AI to create interactive quizzes that transform review sessions into exciting game shows. Students compete against their peers to answer questions correctly and earn points, fostering a sense of healthy competition and boosting engagement with the learning material. AI personalizes the experience by offering students immediate feedback on their responses and adjusting the difficulty level based on their performance.

Leveraging AI for Gamified Learning Experiences

These gamification techniques extend beyond simple quizzes and can be applied to create more immersive and engaging learning experiences for both higher education learners and corporate trainees.

Gamification for Higher Education Learners:

For higher education learners, gamification can be used to enhance engagement in various learning activities beyond quizzes. Here are some specific examples:

- **Case Study Competition:** Imagine a law course where students are divided into teams and compete to develop the strongest legal arguments for a mock trial scenario. AI can be used to score team presentations based on predefined criteria, such as legal accuracy, persuasiveness, and courtroom etiquette. Additionally, AI can analyze student participation within teams, awarding bonus points for active collaboration and knowledge sharing. This gamified approach encourages students to delve deeper into the course material, develop critical thinking and communication skills, and experience the thrill of friendly competition.

- **Gamified Simulations:** For business or healthcare students, AI-powered simulations can create realistic scenarios where students make critical decisions and experience the consequences. These simulations can be gamified by awarding points for making sound decisions based on course content, with leaderboards displaying top performers. For instance, a medical simulation might challenge students to diagnose a virtual patient, incorporating elements of time pressure and limited resources. AI can then evaluate student decisions based on medical best practices and award points accordingly. This type of gamified learning allows students to apply their knowledge in a safe, simulated environment and receive immediate feedback on their decision-making processes.

- **Virtual Escape Rooms:** Escape rooms are a popular team-building activity that can be adapted for higher education. AI can be used to create virtual escape rooms that challenge students to solve problems and collaborate effectively to "escape" within a set time limit. These virtual escape rooms can be designed to reinforce specific course concepts. For example, a history course might offer a virtual escape room where students must decipher historical clues and collaborate to "escape" a virtual recreation of a historical event. This gamified approach fosters critical thinking, collaboration skills, and deeper engagement with the course material.

Gamification for Corporate Learners:

In the corporate world, gamification can be a powerful tool for onboarding new employees, promoting sales training, and encouraging the development of desired skills. Here are some specific examples:

- **Sales Gamification:** Sales training can be gamified by creating a simulated sales environment where trainees compete to close deals with virtual customers. AI can be used to personalize customer interactions based on individual trainee performance, offering more complex scenarios for those who excel in basic sales techniques. Points and leaderboards can be used to motivate trainees and create a healthy sense of competition. This gamified approach allows trainees to practice their sales skills in a safe environment and receive immediate feedback on their communication and negotiation tactics.

- **Leadership Development Games:** Leadership skills can be honed through gamified simulations that present trainees with challenging leadership scenarios. AI can analyze trainee decisions based on pre-defined leadership principles, awarding points for effective communication, delegation, and conflict resolution. Leaderboards can track individual and team performance, fostering a sense of competition and encouraging collaboration. This type of gamified learning experience allows trainees to experiment with different leadership styles, receive feedback on their effectiveness, and develop their leadership potential in a risk-free environment.

- **Onboarding Gamification:** The onboarding process for new employees can be gamified by creating a series of challenges and tasks related to company policies, products, and services. AI can track progress and award badges for completing tasks or achieving milestones. Leaderboards can showcase top performers and encourage friendly competition. This gamified approach transforms the traditional onboarding process into an engaging and interactive experience that helps new employees learn essential information, build relationships with colleagues, and feel more integrated into the company culture.

Case Study: Duolingo and Language Learning Success

Duolingo (https://www.duolingo.com/) exemplifies the power of gamification in language learning. This mobile app utilizes AI to create personalized learning experiences and leverages gamification elements like points, badges, and leaderboards to keep users engaged. Learners earn points for completing lessons, correcting mistakes, and maintaining daily streaks. Leaderboards allow users to compare their progress with friends or compete against a global community. This gamified approach injects a sense of fun and competition into language learning, motivating users to return to the app daily and practice their language skills consistently.

However, it's important to acknowledge that Duolingo, like any educational tool, has its limitations. While it can effectively teach basic vocabulary and grammar structures, fluency requires immersion in a real-world language environment and practicing speaking and listening comprehension skills. Nevertheless, Duolingo serves as a valuable springboard for language learning, and its gamified approach demonstrates the potential of AI to make education not only effective but also engaging and enjoyable.

Continuing the AI Revolution

The exploration of AI in classroom management and student engagement is an ongoing conversation. As AI technology continues to evolve, we can expect even more innovative tools and applications to emerge. Here are some key areas for future exploration:

- **The Role of AI in Social-Emotional Learning:** Can AI be harnessed to create personalized interventions and support systems to address students' social and emotional well-being?

- **AI-powered Assessment and Feedback:** Can AI provide educators and trainers with more nuanced and actionable insights into student or trainee learning, allowing for more effective feedback and personalized instruction?

- **The Ethical Considerations of AI in Education:** As AI plays a more prominent role in education, it's crucial to address issues of bias, transparency, and student privacy. How can we ensure that AI is used ethically and responsibly in learning environments?

By fostering collaboration between educators, trainers, researchers, AI developers, and policymakers, we can harness the power of AI to create a future where learning is not only efficient and effective but also engaging, personalized, and empowering for all.

Even now, AI is poised to transform the way we manage classrooms and training rooms, fostering deeper student engagement across all learning demographics. By harnessing the power of AI responsibly and ethically, we can create learning environments that are:

- **Personalized:** AI can tailor learning experiences to individual student or trainee needs and learning styles, ensuring everyone is challenged appropriately and supported to reach their full potential.

- **Engaging:** AI-powered tools and games can make learning fun and interactive, motivating students and trainees to actively participate in the learning process.

- **Efficient:** AI can automate routine tasks, freeing up valuable educator and trainer time for more personalized instruction and interaction with learners.

- **Inclusive:** AI can be used to create accessible learning materials and provide targeted support for students and trainees with diverse needs.

- **Data-driven:** AI can provide educators and trainers with valuable data and insights into student or trainee progress, allowing them to make informed decisions and adjust their teaching or training strategies accordingly.

As Nelson Mandela aptly stated, "Education is the most powerful weapon which you can use to change the world." By embracing AI as a tool for educational innovation, we can empower educators, trainers, students, and trainees, equipping them with the knowledge, skills, and critical thinking abilities necessary to thrive in the 21st century and build a brighter future for all.

Reflection Questions

For Educators and Trainers:

- How can you leverage AI tools to create a more personalized and engaging learning environment for your students or trainees?

- What ethical considerations need to be addressed when deploying AI tools in your classroom or training room?

- How can you ensure that AI complements your teaching or training practice and doesn't replace the human touch?

For School Administrators, Training Managers, and Policymakers:

- What steps can you take to ensure that educators and trainers receive adequate training and support to integrate AI tools effectively?

- How can you foster collaboration between educators, trainers, developers, and policymakers to promote the responsible and ethical use of AI in learning environments?

- What policies and frameworks need to be in place to safeguard student and trainee privacy and prevent algorithmic bias in AI-powered educational and training tools?

For AI Developers:

- How can you design AI tools that are specifically tailored to the needs of educators, trainers, students, and trainees?

- How can you ensure that your AI tools are transparent and explainable, and promote inclusivity in the classroom or training room?

- How can you collaborate with educators, trainers, researchers, and learners to develop AI tools that foster critical thinking skills alongside content mastery?

By critically reflecting on these questions and working together, we can harness the power of AI to create a future where education and training are not only effective but also engaging, personalized, and empowering for all learners.

Chapter 5: AI and the Transformation of Learning

The world of education is undergoing a revolution fueled by the relentless march of technology. From interactive whiteboards to virtual reality simulations and artificial intelligence (AI), a plethora of groundbreaking tools are emerging to reshape how students learn, and educators teach. This chapter delves into the exciting possibilities and complex challenges that lie ahead in the ever-evolving realm of educational technology (EdTech).

Tailoring AI for Diverse Learning Needs

AI isn't a one-size-fits-all solution. Its effectiveness hinges on customization to meet the specific needs of each learner. Here's a detailed exploration of how AI can be adapted to support students with various learning styles and requirements:

- **Personalized Learning Paths for Students with Dyslexia:** Students with dyslexia often grapple with reading fluency and comprehension due to challenges processing written language. AI-powered tools can analyze a student's reading patterns and pinpoint areas of weakness. Based on this data, AI can personalize learning paths that incorporate features like text-to-speech conversion, dyslexia-friendly fonts, and vocabulary scaffolding. These tools empower students with dyslexia to access learning materials and enhance their reading comprehension skills.

- **AI-powered Assistive Technologies for Students with Visual Impairments:** Students with visual impairments require specialized tools and techniques to access educational content. AI can be harnessed to develop intelligent screen readers that not only convert text to speech but also describe images and graphics in detail. Additionally, AI-powered object recognition tools can be used to help students with visual impairments navigate their surroundings and interact with the physical world more independently.

- **AI-driven Interventions for Students with Autism Spectrum Disorder (ASD):** Social interaction and communication can be challenging for students with ASD. AI-powered virtual tutors can provide personalized social skills training in a safe and controlled environment. These virtual tutors can utilize AI to analyze student responses and provide real-time feedback, helping students develop social-emotional skills and communication strategies.

- **AI Tools to Support Students with Attention Deficit Hyperactivity Disorder (ADHD):** Students with ADHD often struggle with focus and staying on task. AI-powered learning management systems can be used to create personalized learning schedules with built-in breaks and reminders. Gamification elements like points, badges, and leaderboards can be incorporated into learning activities to keep students with ADHD engaged and motivated. Additionally, AI can analyze student behavior patterns and identify potential distractions, allowing educators to implement targeted interventions and strategies to improve focus and concentration.

AI and Inclusive Education: Breaking Down Barriers

Inclusive education strives to provide all students with a quality education, regardless of their abilities. AI has the potential to be a powerful tool for promoting inclusivity and ensuring accessibility for students with diverse needs. Here's a closer look at how AI can contribute to a more inclusive learning environment:

- **Shattering Communication Barriers:** AI-powered language translation tools can be used to translate lectures, course materials, and classroom discussions into real-time, allowing students who speak different languages to participate fully in the learning process. Additionally, AI can be used to develop sign language recognition software that translates spoken language into sign language for students who are deaf or hard of hearing.

- **Personalized Learning for Students with Diverse Needs:** As discussed earlier, AI can be used to create personalized learning paths that cater to the specific needs of each student. This is particularly beneficial for students with disabilities, ensuring they receive targeted instruction and support to achieve their learning goals. AI-powered adaptive learning platforms can adjust the difficulty level of learning materials based on student performance, providing appropriate challenges and preventing frustration for students who may learn at a different pace than their peers.

- **Promoting Student Independence:** AI-powered assistive technologies can empower students with disabilities to become more independent learners. Tools like voice-activated controls, text-to-speech conversion, and screen readers can allow students to access information and complete tasks without requiring constant assistance. This fosters a sense of autonomy and self-confidence in students with disabilities.

Case Studies: AI in Action

Seeing AI in action within the classroom solidifies its potential benefits. Here are a couple of real-world examples showcasing how AI is being used to support students with disabilities:

Case Study 1: Seeing Institute's AI-powered Reading Tutor: The Seeing Clearly Institute, a non-profit organization dedicated to helping individuals with visual impairments, has developed an AI-powered reading tutor specifically designed for students with low vision. This tutor utilizes a combination of text-to-speech conversion, object recognition, and real-time feedback to guide students through reading activities and improve their reading comprehension skills. The AI tutor personalizes the reading experience by adjusting the font size, color contrast, and reading pace based on each student's individual needs.

Case Study 2: Lexia Learning's Personalized Reading Interventions Powered by AI

Lexia Learning, a leading provider of educational technology solutions, utilizes AI to personalize reading interventions for students with dyslexia and other reading difficulties. Their flagship program, Lexia PowerUp, employs AI algorithms to analyze student performance data and identify areas where each student needs the most support.

Here's a breakdown of how Lexia PowerUp leverages AI to support students with dyslexia:

- **Adaptive Learning Approach:** Lexia PowerUp utilizes an adaptive learning engine that tailors the learning experience to each student's individual needs. The AI analyzes student responses in real time and adjusts the difficulty level of reading exercises, vocabulary instruction, and phonics practice accordingly. This ensures that students are challenged appropriately, neither feeling frustrated by overly difficult material nor bored by repetitive exercises.

- **Personalized Phonics Instruction:** Students with dyslexia often struggle with phonics, the relationship between letters and sounds. Lexia PowerUp utilizes AI to personalize phonics instruction based on each student's specific challenges. The program identifies areas of weakness, such as difficulty with consonant blends or vowel sounds, and delivers targeted instruction to address those specific needs.

- **Engaging Activities and Gamification:** Lexia PowerUp recognizes that effective learning should be engaging. The program utilizes AI to create interactive reading activities and games that cater to students' learning styles. Gamification elements like points, badges, and leaderboards motivate students to complete reading exercises and keep them engaged in the learning process.

- **Real-time Progress Monitoring:** Educators and parents need clear data to track student progress and assess the effectiveness of interventions. Lexia PowerUp provides real-time progress reports generated by AI algorithms. These reports provide detailed information on student performance, areas of strength and weakness, and progress over time. This data allows educators to personalize instruction further and adjust interventions as needed.

The success stories of the Seeing Clearly Institute and Lexia Learning demonstrate the real-world impact AI can have on students with special needs. By personalizing learning, promoting accessibility, and providing educators with valuable data, AI holds immense potential to transform the landscape of special education and empower all students to reach their full potential.

AI for Higher Education and Corporate Training

The impact of AI extends beyond special education, transforming learning experiences in higher education and corporate training environments as well. Here are some examples of how AI is being tailored to these settings:

- **Personalized Learning Paths in Higher Education:** Similar to its application for students with dyslexia, AI can personalize learning journeys for students in higher education. By analyzing a student's progress in areas like vocabulary acquisition, problem-solving skills, and critical thinking abilities, AI can recommend personalized learning activities and resources. This could include targeted practice problems in STEM fields, curated historical documents for research papers, or interactive simulations for complex scientific concepts.

- **AI-powered Writing Tutors Across Disciplines:** AI-powered writing tutors can be invaluable for students across all disciplines in higher education. These tutors can analyze student essays, research papers, and other written assignments, providing feedback on grammar, clarity, structure, and even citation formatting. Additionally, AI tutors can offer suggestions for relevant academic sources and help students strengthen their arguments and writing styles specific to their field of study.

- **AI-driven Assessment and Feedback:** AI can go beyond static multiple-choice tests. AI-powered assessment tools can analyze student responses to open-ended questions, essays, and projects, providing more nuanced feedback and identifying areas where students may need additional support. This allows educators to tailor their instruction and interventions more effectively. For instance, AI can analyze an essay written for a history course and identify weaknesses in historical context or source utilization, prompting the instructor to provide targeted resources and guidance.

Transforming Corporate Training with AI:

- **AI for Soft Skills Development in Corporate Training:** Soft skills, such as communication, collaboration, and problem-solving, are crucial for success in today's ever-changing workplace. AI-powered simulations can create realistic scenarios where employees can practice soft skills in a safe and controlled environment. For instance, an AI-driven virtual reality simulation could place a salesperson in a challenging customer interaction, allowing them to practice negotiation tactics and communication strategies in a risk-free environment. AI can then provide feedback on the employee's performance, identifying areas for improvement and suggesting targeted training modules.

- **Personalized Onboarding Experiences for New Hires:** The onboarding process sets new hires up for success. AI can personalize the onboarding experience by creating individualized learning paths based on the new hire's role, prior experience, and knowledge gaps. This could include bite-sized eLearning modules on company policies and procedures, interactive simulations specific to the company's products or services, personalized coaching from senior colleagues, or AI-powered chatbots that can answer frequently asked questions 24/7.

- **AI-powered Microlearning for Continuous Skill Development:** In today's dynamic business landscape, continuous learning is essential for employees to stay up to date with industry trends and technologies. AI can be used to create microlearning modules, which are short, focused learning experiences delivered on demand through mobile devices or learning management systems. These microlearning modules can address specific skill gaps identified through performance assessments or employee feedback, ensuring employees have the knowledge and skills they need to perform their jobs effectively.

For example, an AI system in a marketing department might identify a knowledge gap in social media advertising best practices. It could then recommend a series of microlearning modules tailored to the specific needs of the employees, ensuring they are equipped with the latest strategies and techniques for success.

By personalizing learning experiences, providing educators and trainers with valuable data-driven insights, and fostering a more engaging learning environment, AI has the potential to revolutionize the way knowledge and skills are acquired across all educational and training sectors. However, it's crucial to remember that AI is a tool, and its effectiveness hinges on responsible implementation with careful consideration of ethical concerns.

The Ethical Considerations of AI in Learning

While AI offers a wealth of opportunities in education and training, ethical considerations need to be addressed to ensure its responsible and equitable implementation. Here are some key points to ponder:

- **Algorithmic Bias:** AI algorithms are only as good as the data they are trained on. If training data contains biases, these biases can be reflected in the AI's outputs. In the context of education and training, this could lead to AI tools that unintentionally disadvantage certain student or employee populations. It's crucial to ensure that AI algorithms are developed and trained with diverse data sets to mitigate bias and ensure fair outcomes for all learners.

- **Privacy Concerns:** The use of AI in education and training raises concerns about student and employee data privacy. As AI tools collect and analyze data, it's essential to have robust data security measures in place to protect privacy and ensure that data is used ethically and responsibly.

- **Over-reliance on Technology:** AI should be seen as a tool to empower educators and trainers, not replace them. The human touch remains invaluable in education and training settings. Educators and trainers need to be involved in selecting and implementing AI tools, ensuring they complement existing instructional practices and foster a positive learning environment for all learners.

By carefully considering these ethical considerations, we can harness the power of AI responsibly and ensure that it serves as a force for positive change in all educational and training environments.

The Future of AI in Learning: A Glimpse into Emerging Trends

The realm of AI in learning is constantly evolving, with new advancements and applications emerging on the horizon. Here's a look at some intriguing trends that could shape the future of education and training:

- **AI-powered Personalized Learning Ecosystems:** Imagine a future where AI curates a comprehensive learning ecosystem tailored to each individual's unique needs and preferences. This ecosystem could encompass a blend of online resources, adaptive learning platforms, virtual reality simulations, and personalized interactions with AI tutors and human educators.

61

AI would continuously analyze a learner's progress, interests, and learning style, dynamically adjusting the learning environment to optimize knowledge acquisition and skill development.

- **The Rise of Intelligent Virtual Learning Companions:** AI-powered virtual companions could become ubiquitous in learning environments, offering personalized guidance, support, and encouragement. These companions could act as intelligent tutors, study partners, and even motivational coaches, adapting their interactions based on the learner's emotional state and progress. Imagine a virtual companion celebrating a student's success in mastering a challenging concept or offering words of encouragement when facing a learning obstacle.

- **Gamification on Steroids: Immersive Learning with AR and VR:** The future of learning could be infused with a healthy dose of fun and engagement through the integration of augmented reality (AR) and virtual reality (VR) technologies. AI could power these immersive learning experiences, creating interactive simulations and scenarios that allow learners to explore complex concepts and practice skills in a safe and realistic environment. Imagine a medical student performing a virtual surgery or a history student being transported back in time to witness a historical event unfold – all facilitated by AI-powered AR/VR experiences.

- **The Democratization of Education with AI-powered Language Translation:** Language barriers should not impede access to quality education. AI-powered language translation tools have the potential to break down these barriers, enabling seamless communication and knowledge exchange across cultures. Real-time translation of lectures, course materials, and discussions could create a more inclusive learning environment for students with diverse linguistic backgrounds.

Conclusion: The Human-AI Partnership in Learning

The future of learning is not about AI replacing educators and trainers, but rather about fostering a powerful human-AI partnership. AI can handle the heavy lifting of data analysis, personalization, and intelligent feedback generation, while educators can focus on the irreplaceable aspects of human interaction, motivation, and fostering a love of learning. By embracing AI as a valuable tool and addressing ethical considerations responsibly, we can create a future where learning is more personalized, engaging, and accessible for all.

This chapter has explored the immense potential of AI in transforming the learning landscape. From personalizing learning experiences for students with disabilities to revolutionizing corporate training programs, AI offers a plethora of exciting possibilities. As we move forward, it's crucial to ensure the responsible development and implementation of AI in learning, keeping ethical considerations at the forefront and ensuring that AI serves as a tool to empower educators, trainers, and learners alike.

Reflection Questions for Chapter 5: AI and the Transformation of Learning

To solidify your understanding of the intricate relationship between AI and the future of learning, consider the following thought-provoking questions:

Tailoring AI for Diverse Learning Needs:

- Consider a specific learning challenge faced by students (e.g., dyslexia, ADHD). How can AI be tailored to address this challenge and personalize the learning experience?

- What potential benefits and drawbacks do you see in using AI-powered assistive technologies in education?

The Impact of AI on Inclusive Education and Accessibility:

- How can AI be leveraged to create a more inclusive learning environment for students with diverse needs?

- Think about the challenges faced by students who speak different languages in a classroom setting. How can AI-powered language translation tools address these challenges and promote equitable access to education?

Case Studies: AI in Action:

- Read more about the Seeing Clearly Institute's AI-powered reading tutor and Lexia Learning's Lexia PowerUp program. What specific features of these programs do you find most promising for supporting students with reading difficulties?

- Can you identify similar AI applications being used in your own educational background or workplace training? How have they impacted the learning experience?

AI for Higher Education and Corporate Training:

- Imagine you are a course instructor in your field of study. How could AI be used to personalize the learning experience for your students?

- Consider the concept of microlearning modules in corporate training. How can AI be used to develop effective microlearning modules that address specific skill gaps identified among employees?

The Ethical Considerations of AI in Learning:

- What are the potential risks associated with algorithmic bias in AI-powered educational tools? How can we mitigate these risks and ensure fair outcomes for all learners?

- How can we ensure data privacy and security when using AI tools that collect and analyze student or employee data in educational and training settings?

The Future of AI in Learning: A Glimpse into Emerging Trends:

- The chapter discusses the concept of AI-powered personalized learning ecosystems. Describe your vision for what such an ecosystem might look like and how it could benefit learners.

- How can AI-powered virtual learning companions enhance the learning experience and provide additional support for students?

- Imagine the possibilities of using AR and VR technologies powered by AI in education and training. Describe a specific learning scenario that could be revolutionized by these immersive experiences.

By critically reflecting on these questions, you can gain a deeper understanding of the potential and challenges associated with AI in learning. Consider how AI can be harnessed responsibly to create a more personalized, engaging, and accessible learning environment for all. As we stand at the precipice of this transformative era in education, let's embrace AI as a collaborative partner, ensuring it empowers educators, trainers, and learners alike to navigate the exciting frontiers of knowledge acquisition and skill development.

Chapter 6: AI-powered Assessment and Feedback: Revolutionizing Learning Measurement in Executive Education and Higher Learning

The once-static realm of learning assessment is undergoing a paradigm shift. Fueled by the relentless march of artificial intelligence (AI), a new era of dynamic and data-driven evaluation methods is emerging. This chapter delves into the transformative potential of AI for both executive education programs and higher learning institutions. We'll explore how these institutions can leverage AI to automate tedious tasks, deliver real-time feedback, and gain deeper insights into student learning, ultimately fostering a more personalized and effective learning experience.

Automating and Streamlining Assessment Processes with AI

Traditionally, assessments in executive education and higher learning have relied heavily on standardized tests, essays, and subjective faculty evaluations. These methods, while established, are often plagued by limitations. Time constraints restrict the breadth and depth of assessment, subjective evaluations can lack consistency, and manual grading can be a laborious and error-prone process. AI offers a compelling solution, automating tedious tasks and providing a more nuanced picture of student learning.

AI-powered Automated Grading and Scoring:

Repetitive tasks like grading multiple-choice questions, short-answer responses, and even essays can be significantly streamlined with AI. Algorithms trained on vast datasets can efficiently grade these assessments with a high degree of accuracy, freeing up valuable faculty time for more strategic endeavors.

1. Executive Education Example: Pre-program Assessments

Many executive education programs employ pre-program assessments to gauge participants' baseline knowledge and tailor learning experiences. AI-powered grading tools can efficiently process these pre-assessments, allowing program administrators to quickly identify areas where participants might need additional support or targeted instruction. This facilitates a more personalized learning journey from the outset.

Higher Learning Example: High-volume Introductory Courses

Large introductory courses in higher learning often involve grading a significant volume of student work. AI-powered grading tools can be a valuable asset, reducing the faculty workload and ensuring consistent application of grading rubrics.

2. Adaptive Assessments: Dynamic Learning Paths

One of the most exciting applications of AI in assessment lies in its ability to create adaptive assessments. These assessments dynamically adjust the difficulty level of questions in real time based on a student's performance. This personalized approach ensures high-performing students are challenged with more complex material, while those facing difficulties receive targeted support.

Executive Education Example: Personalized Learning Plans

Executive education participants often come from diverse backgrounds with varying levels of prior knowledge. AI-powered adaptive assessments can be used to create personalized learning plans, tailoring the curriculum to each participant's individual needs. This ensures that participants gain the most value from their learning experience, focusing on areas where they can achieve the most significant growth.

Higher Learning Example: Targeted Remediation

In higher learning settings, adaptive assessments can be used to identify areas where students might be struggling. Based on assessment data, the AI can recommend targeted remedial exercises or additional resources to bridge knowledge gaps and ensure all students progress through the course material effectively.

Considerations: While AI-powered grading and adaptive assessments offer significant benefits, it's crucial to remember that human expertise remains valuable. Faculty should utilize AI as a tool to streamline workflows and gain data-driven insights, but the nuanced feedback and critical thinking skills imparted by human educators remain irreplaceable.

Reflection Questions:

- How could your institution leverage AI-powered grading and adaptive assessments to improve the efficiency and effectiveness of learning programs?

- What potential challenges might arise when implementing AI-powered assessments? How can these challenges be mitigated?

Further Exploration:

Investigate existing AI-powered assessment platforms and tools designed for adult learners and higher education institutions.

Consider how these tools could be integrated into your program offerings.

The Role of AI in Providing Real-Time Feedback: Fostering Dynamic Learning Environments

Feedback is the cornerstone of effective learning. It allows students to identify strengths and weaknesses, adjust their learning strategies, and solidify their understanding of concepts. Traditionally, feedback mechanisms in executive education and higher learning have often been delayed, with students receiving evaluations after completing assessments or assignments. AI offers a transformative approach, enabling real-time feedback that fosters a more dynamic and interactive learning environment.

1. AI-powered Formative Assessment Tools: Continuous Improvement

Formative assessments, unlike summative assessments which measure final learning outcomes, provide feedback throughout the learning process. AI-powered formative assessment tools can be seamlessly embedded within online learning platforms, executive education modules, or even in-person classroom experiences. As students engage in learning activities like quizzes, simulations, or interactive exercises, they receive immediate feedback on their performance. This allows them to course-correct and refine their understanding as they learn, ultimately fostering a deeper level of engagement with the material.

Executive Education Example: Case Study Analysis and Discussion

Executive education programs often utilize case studies to stimulate critical thinking and problem-solving skills. Traditionally, faculty facilitate post-analysis discussions to offer feedback on student approaches. However, AI-powered formative assessment tools can facilitate real-time feedback during these discussions. For instance, an AI system could analyze student contributions, identifying potential biases, incomplete analyses, or missed opportunities. This real-time feedback loop allows participants to refine their arguments and benefit from collective learning experiences more effectively.

Higher Learning Example: Interactive Online Courses with Embedded Formative Assessments

In higher learning institutions, AI-powered formative assessments can be embedded within online courses to provide students with immediate feedback on their progress. This continuous feedback loop ensures students are on the right track and can address any knowledge gaps early on. For example, an interactive online biology course could utilize AI to analyze student responses in a simulation modeling population growth. If a student's model yields unexpected results, the AI could provide real-time prompts or resources to help them identify and correct errors in their understanding of ecological principles.

2. AI-powered Personalized Coaching: Beyond Standardized Feedback

Traditionally, feedback in executive education and higher learning has often been standardized and delivered through rubrics or written evaluations. While these methods have merit, they can sometimes lack the nuance necessary for true growth. AI offers the potential to personalize feedback, tailoring it to individual student strengths, weaknesses, and learning styles.

Executive Education Example: Personalized Feedback on Leadership Simulations

Many executive education programs incorporate leadership simulations to assess decision-making skills and strategic thinking. AI-powered coaching tools can analyze a participant's performance within the simulation, identifying areas where they excelled and pinpointing areas for improvement. This personalized feedback goes beyond generic rubrics, allowing participants to receive targeted insights into their leadership strengths and areas for development.

Higher Learning Example: AI-powered Writing Tutors for Personalized Feedback

Writing skills are crucial across many disciplines in higher learning. AI-powered writing tutors can analyze student essays, research papers, and other written assignments, providing personalized feedback on grammar, clarity, structure, and even citation formatting. This AI-driven analysis can then be supplemented by faculty input, allowing students to receive a comprehensive overview of their writing strengths and specific areas for improvement.

Considerations: While real-time feedback provides immediate benefits, it's important to ensure it is delivered constructively and doesn't overwhelm learners. Additionally, the human touch remains irreplaceable. AI-powered feedback should be viewed as a tool to empower instructors, not replace them.

Reflection Questions:

- How could your institution leverage AI-powered formative assessment tools and personalized coaching to enhance the learning experience for students?

- What potential ethical considerations need to be addressed when implementing AI-powered real-time feedback mechanisms?

Further Exploration:

Investigate existing AI-powered coaching platforms and writing feedback tools designed for adult learners and higher education institutions. Consider how these tools could be integrated into your program offerings or course design.

Throughout this chapter, we've explored how AI can revolutionize assessment and feedback in executive education and higher learning. By leveraging AI to automate tedious tasks, deliver real-time feedback, and gain deeper insights into student learning, institutions can create a more personalized and effective learning experience for all.

Bonus Assessment

AI in Learning Management Systems: A Needs Assessment (Likert Scale)

This assessment is designed to help companies and higher education institutions evaluate their current learning management systems (LMS) and determine the potential benefits of integrating AI functionalities. Responses are based on a 5-point Likert scale, with 1 representing "Strongly Disagree" and 5 representing "Strongly Agree."

Part 1: Company Assessment

Employee Engagement and Learning (10 Questions):

1. To what extent do employees complete assigned learning modules within your LMS? (1 - Rarely, 5 - Consistently) *
   Outcome: Low scores indicate low engagement, suggesting AI-powered personalized learning paths could be beneficial.

2. How satisfied are your employees with the variety of learning materials offered through your LMS? (1 - Very Dissatisfied, 5 - Very Satisfied) * **Outcome:** Low satisfaction suggests a need for AI to curate and recommend relevant learning materials for individual employees.

3. How effective is your current LMS in tracking individual employee progress through learning modules? (1 - Not Effective at All, 5 - Highly Effective) * **Outcome:** Low effectiveness points towards the potential benefit of AI-powered progress tracking with detailed learning analytics.

4. How often do employees interact with quizzes, discussions, or other interactive features within your LMS courses? (1 - Never, 5 - Frequently) * **Outcome:** Infrequent interaction suggests a need for AI to personalize learning content and increase interactivity.

5. On a scale of 1 to 5, how satisfied are your employees with the feedback mechanisms within your LMS? (1 - Very Dissatisfied, 5 - Very Satisfied) * **Outcome:** Low satisfaction indicates a potential benefit for AI-powered feedback that is personalized and actionable.

6. How well does your current LMS cater to the diverse learning styles of your employees? (1 - Not at All, 5 - Extremely Well) * **Outcome:** Low scores suggest a need for AI to personalize learning based on individual styles (visual, auditory, kinesthetic).

7. To what extent do employees feel their current LMS learning experiences translate into improved job performance? (1 - Not at All, 5 - Significantly) * **Outcome:** Low scores suggest a benefit for AI to tailor learning content to specific job roles and skills gaps.

8. How often do employees abandon LMS learning modules due to a lack of clarity or relevance? (1 - Never, 5 - Frequently) * **Outcome:** Frequent abandonment suggests a need for AI to recommend more relevant learning paths based on employee needs.

9. On average, how much time does your HR department spend on administrative tasks related to LMS management (enrollments, assignments, reporting)? (1 - Minimal Time, 5 - Significant Time) * **Outcome:** High time spent on administrative tasks indicates a potential benefit for AI automation.

10. How confident are you that your current LMS provides valuable data and insights into employee learning and development needs? (1 - Not Confident at All, 5 - Highly Confident) * **Outcome:** Low confidence suggests a potential benefit for AI to generate more comprehensive data and actionable insights.

Part 2: Higher Education Assessment

Student Learning and Assessment (10 Questions):

1. How satisfied are your faculty with the current ease of use and user interface of your LMS? (1 - Very Dissatisfied, 5 - Very Satisfied) * **Outcome:** Low satisfaction suggests a need for AI to streamline faculty workflows and improve LMS usability.

2. To what extent do your current LMS assessment methods provide a comprehensive picture of student learning? (1 - Not at All, 5 - Extremely Well) * **Outcome:** Low scores suggest a benefit for AI-powered adaptive assessments that measure diverse learning objectives.

3. How effective is your current LMS in providing faculty with detailed data on student performance within courses? (1 - Not Effective at All, 5 - Highly Effective) * **Outcome:** Low effectiveness suggests a need for AI to generate data visualizations and insights to inform instructional decisions.

4. On average, how much time do faculty spend on grading essays, quizzes, and other student assessments? (1 - Minimal Time, 5 - Significant Time) * **Outcome:** High time spent on grading indicates a potential benefit for AI-powered automated grading and scoring tools.

5. How satisfied are your students with the current level of personalized feedback they receive on their LMS assignments? (1 - Very Dissatisfied, 5 - Very Satisfied) * **Outcome:** Low satisfaction suggests a need for AI to analyze student work and provide personalized feedback beyond generic rubrics.

6. To what extent does your LMS support the use of interactive learning tools (simulations, gamified activities) within courses? (1 - Not at All, 5 - Extensively) * **Outcome:** Low support suggests a need for AI to recommend and integrate interactive learning experiences that enhance student engagement.

7. How confident are your instructors in their ability to provide timely and personalized feedback to all students? (1 - Not Confident at All, 5 - Highly Confident) * **Outcome:** Low confidence suggests a benefit for AI to assist with automated feedback mechanisms and flag areas where students might need individual instructor attention.

8. How satisfied are your students with the current accessibility features offered by your LMS (e.g., text-to-speech, captioning)? (1 - Very Dissatisfied, 5 - Very Satisfied) *

Outcome: Low satisfaction suggests a need for AI to personalize learning experiences to cater to diverse student needs and learning styles.

9. On average, how many hours per week does your faculty spend on administrative tasks related to LMS course management (content creation, student enrollment, gradebook management)? (1 - 0-2 hours, 5 - 5+ hours) * **Outcome:** High time spent on administrative tasks suggests a need for AI to automate repetitive tasks and streamline faculty workflows.

10. How well does your LMS provide data and insights to help advisors personalize student learning pathways? (1 - Not Helpful at All, 5 - Extremely Helpful) * **Outcome:** Low scores suggest a benefit for AI to analyze student data and recommend personalized learning paths based on individual strengths and weaknesses.

Analysis:

Companies and institutions with a high average score (above 4) in the satisfaction sections and low average scores (below 3) in the effectiveness sections are likely functioning well with their current LMS. However, those with lower satisfaction scores and higher time commitments on administrative tasks might benefit significantly from exploring AI integration within their LMS. AI can automate repetitive tasks, personalize learning experiences, and offer real-time feedback mechanisms, all of which can contribute to increased employee/student engagement and improved learning outcomes.

Next Steps:

Based on your assessment results, consider researching specific AI-powered LMS functionalities that address your identified needs. Pilot programs and demonstrations can help you evaluate the effectiveness of AI integration in your learning environment. Remember, AI should be viewed as a tool to empower instructors and personalize learning, not replace human interaction and expertise.

Chapter 7: The AI-Enhanced Classroom: A Conductor's Guide for Higher Education and Executive Training

The traditional model of higher education and executive training is undergoing a transformation driven by artificial intelligence (AI). Similar to how an orchestra conductor leads a complex musical piece, instructors have long shouldered the weight of content delivery, assessment, and individualized instruction. AI presents a compelling opportunity to share this workload, freeing up valuable instructor time for more strategic endeavors. This chapter explores how AI empowers instructors in higher education and executive training, ultimately leading to improved student/participant productivity and a stronger return on investment (ROI) for organizations.

The AI Advantage: Boosting Productivity and ROI.

While the core responsibilities of instructors remain vital, AI can significantly enhance their effectiveness. Let's explore how AI empowers higher education and executive training by:

- **From Knowledge Delivery to Personalized Learning Architects:** Instructors can leverage AI to automate routine tasks like delivering foundational lectures. This frees them to focus on crafting personalized learning experiences. Imagine a business management course where AI delivers core lectures on key financial concepts. The instructor can then use AI-powered adaptive learning platforms to tailor the curriculum to individual needs. Students who grasp financial ratios can delve deeper into advanced analysis tools, while those who struggle with basic concepts receive targeted support and resources. This personalized approach fosters deeper understanding and engagement, ultimately enhancing student/participant productivity in their chosen field.

Example: AI-powered Learning Management Systems with Adaptive Learning Modules

A university business program utilizes an AI-powered Learning Management System (LMS) with adaptive learning modules. The LMS delivers introductory video lectures on finance fundamentals. Following each lecture, the AI system analyzes student performance on quizzes and assignments. Based on this data, the LMS recommends individualized learning pathways for each student. Students who excel receive advanced modules on financial modeling, while those who struggle receive targeted video tutorials and practice exercises.

- **From Grading Drudgery to Real-Time Insights and Actionable Feedback:** AI algorithms can efficiently grade multiple-choice questions, short-answer responses, and even essays. This frees instructors to dedicate more time to providing personalized feedback that goes beyond grades. Imagine an executive training program where AI grades individual and team project reports. The instructor can then analyze AI-generated reports that identify areas where teams excelled in collaborative strategy or struggled with project management. This allows for targeted feedback sessions that focus on improvement and equip participants with actionable skills to benefit their organizations.

Example: AI-powered Automated Grading with Team Performance Reports

An executive training program on leadership and team management utilizes AI for automated grading of team project deliverables. The AI system analyzes reports, identifying areas where teams demonstrated effective communication and collaborative problem-solving. The instructor then reviews the reports and utilizes the AI-generated insights to tailor feedback sessions for each team. These sessions highlight team strengths and offer constructive criticism, allowing participants to hone their leadership skills and translate them into improved team performance back at their companies.

- **From Static Assessments to Dynamic Learning Support and Continuous Improvement:** AI-powered adaptive assessments can dynamically adjust the difficulty level of questions based on individual performance. This allows instructors to identify knowledge gaps and tailor instruction accordingly. Imagine a data science course where an AI system administers adaptive quizzes. Students who excel at statistical analysis receive more complex problems, while those who struggle with basic concepts receive targeted review materials and additional practice opportunities. This continuous assessment and adaptation ensure that all participants are challenged and supported throughout the learning journey, maximizing their knowledge acquisition and ultimately their ROI in terms of career advancement.

Example: AI-powered Adaptive Quizzes with Targeted Review Materials

A graduate program in data science utilizes an AI system to administer adaptive quizzes on machine learning algorithms. Students who answer questions correctly receive quizzes with more complex algorithms, while those who encounter difficulties receive immediate access to relevant video tutorials and practice problems based on the identified knowledge gaps. This dynamic approach ensures all students progress at their own pace, ultimately fostering a deeper understanding of data science concepts and a stronger return on investment for their tuition fees.

Considerations: While AI offers a multitude of benefits, the human touch is irreplaceable. Instructors remain essential for facilitating discussions, fostering critical thinking skills, and inspiring participants. AI should be viewed as a valuable tool to empower instructors, not as a substitute for their expertise.

The Importance of Effective Instructional Design:

Leveraging the full potential of AI in higher education and executive training requires a focus on effective instructional design. Instructors need to be trained on how to:

- Integrate AI tools seamlessly into their curriculum.

- Develop personalized learning pathways based on AI-generated data and student/participant performance.

- Design engaging learning activities that leverage AI-powered simulations and case studies.

- Craft effective prompts for personalized feedback using AI insights.

By focusing on these areas, instructors can become skilled conductors in the AI-enhanced learning environment, leading to a more advanced learning experience.

Here are some additional aspects of effective instructional design in the AI-enhanced classroom:

- **Focus on Active Learning:** While AI can deliver foundational knowledge, instructors should design learning experiences that encourage active participation. This might involve incorporating case studies, group discussions, and simulations that leverage AI-powered features. Imagine a law school course where students use AI-powered simulations to practice legal arguments in different courtroom scenarios. This active learning approach not only reinforces theoretical knowledge but also hones critical thinking and communication skills, essential for success in the legal field.

- **Curate High-Quality Learning Materials:** AI can assist instructors in identifying relevant and up-to-date learning materials. However, the responsibility for curation ultimately falls on the instructor. This ensures that the learning experience is comprehensive, integrates diverse perspectives, and aligns with the overall course objectives.

- **Foster Human Connection and Collaboration:** While AI personalized learning, it cannot replicate the value of human interaction. Instructors should design activities that encourage collaboration, peer-to-peer learning, and the exchange of ideas. This fosters a sense of community and allows participants to learn from each other's experiences.

Building the Skills for the AI Age: Training and Development for Instructors

The successful integration of AI into higher education and executive training hinges on equipping instructors with the knowledge and skills necessary to leverage its potential effectively. Here's how professional development programs can help instructors become proficient conductors in the AI age:

- **Building AI Literacy:** Instructors need a foundational understanding of AI capabilities and limitations. Training programs can deconstruct AI terminology, showcase various AI tools for education and training, and equip instructors with the ability to critically evaluate the potential benefits and ethical considerations of AI-based applications.

Example: AI in Higher Education Workshops

Universities and training organizations can offer workshops designed to build AI literacy among instructors. These workshops could include interactive sessions where instructors explore different AI tools for assessment, personalized learning, curriculum development, and simulation design.

- **Developing Instructional Design Skills for AI-Enhanced Learning:** AI presents new opportunities for innovative instructional design. Professional development programs can equip instructors with the skills to:

    o Design engaging learning experiences that seamlessly integrate AI tools.

    o Analyze and utilize AI-generated data to develop personalized learning pathways.

    o Craft effective prompts for personalized feedback using AI insights.

    o Facilitate active learning experiences like case studies, simulations, and discussions.

Example: AI-Powered Simulation Design for Business Courses

A professional development program offers a workshop on using AI-powered simulations in business courses. Instructors learn how to design simulations that leverage AI to create realistic scenarios for participants to practice negotiation strategies, manage virtual teams, or make data-driven business decisions.

By equipping instructors with the necessary skills and fostering a culture of continuous learning, universities, and training organizations can harness the power of AI to create a more effective and engaging learning environment for students and participants. This ultimately leads to a stronger return on investment (ROI) for both learners and institutions.

Fostering Continuous Learning with AI: A Conductor's Toolkit

Instructors can leverage AI to create an environment that encourages continuous learning beyond the confines of a course. Here are some tips and tricks:

- **AI-Powered Learning Paths:** Utilize AI to analyze student performance and recommend additional learning materials or advanced modules based on individual strengths and weaknesses. This allows students to delve deeper into areas of interest and address any knowledge gaps.

- **Microlearning Modules with Gamification:** Create bite-sized learning modules that can be accessed anytime, anywhere. Integrate gamification elements like badges and leaderboards to keep students engaged and motivated to learn more.

- **AI-Driven Self-Assessments:** Design self-assessments powered by AI that offer personalized feedback and suggest targeted practice activities based on the student's performance. This empowers students to take ownership of their learning journey and continuously improve.

Example: Imagine a history instructor who curates a series of microlearning modules on specific historical events using AI recommendations. Students who excel in a module on the French Revolution can access an advanced module on the Napoleonic Wars. Those who struggle with a particular event can receive personalized practice quizzes and targeted video tutorials.

A Smooth Transition to Lifelong Learning:

By creating and demonstrating a love of learning through personalized experiences and readily available resources, AI in the classroom becomes a springboard for lifelong learning.

Reflection for Higher Ed Students and Administrators:

- **Students:** Embrace AI as a tool to personalize your learning journey. Explore the additional resources and pathways suggested by AI to deepen your understanding and discover new areas of interest.

- **Administrators:** Invest in professional development programs to equip instructors with the skills to leverage AI effectively. Explore partnerships with AI developers to create educational tools tailored to your institution's needs.

Reflection for Corporate Learners:

- **Learners:** Actively participate in AI-powered learning activities and self-assessments. Utilize personalized feedback and learning pathways to continuously upgrade your skill set and stay relevant in the ever-evolving corporate landscape.

- **Corporate Trainers:** Integrate AI-enhanced learning modules into your training programs to provide a more personalized and engaging learning experience for your employees. Utilize AI data to identify knowledge gaps and tailor training programs to address specific needs within your organization.

Conclusion:

By using AI as a conductor's instrument, instructors can create a symphony of learning that empowers students and participants to become lifelong learners and achieve greater success. Higher education institutions and corporations can leverage AI to create a more dynamic and personalized learning experience, ultimately leading to a stronger return on investment for all stakeholders.

Chapter 8: The Ethical and Privacy Implications of AI in Education: Navigating the Symphony's Harmony (Continued)

Delving Deeper: A Look at Specific Ethical Concerns

While the previous section provided a broad overview of ethical considerations, a deeper dive into specific concerns is necessary. Here's a closer look at three key areas:

1. **Privacy and Data Security:**

   o **Student Data Collection and Use:** AI systems often require vast amounts of student data, including test scores, learning patterns, and even biometric information. This raises concerns about the nature of the data collected, its intended use, and the potential for misuse by third parties.

      ■ **Actionable Tips:**

         ■ Implement clear and comprehensive data collection policies that clearly outline the types of data collected, the purpose for collection, and the duration of data storage.

         ■ Obtain explicit consent from students and parents for data collection, ensuring transparency about how data will be used and anonymized whenever possible.

- Partner with reputable AI vendors who prioritize robust data security measures, including encryption and access controls.

2. **Algorithmic Bias and Fairness:**

   o **Biased Data Sets:** AI algorithms are only as good as the data they are trained on. Unfortunately, datasets used to train AI systems can reflect existing societal biases. This can lead to unfair assessments, and biased learning pathways, and ultimately hinder the educational opportunities for certain student groups. For example, an AI-powered reading assessment tool trained on a dataset with a limited representation of minority languages might disadvantage students from those backgrounds.

     - **Actionable Tips:**

       - Conduct thorough audits of AI algorithms to identify potential biases in the training data. This may involve collaborating with diversity, equity, and inclusion (DE&I) experts.

       - Utilize diverse and inclusive datasets that reflect the demographics of the student population. This may require actively seeking out and curating data that represents various cultures, ethnicities, and learning styles.

       - Develop clear guidelines and protocols for mitigating bias in AI-powered education tools. These guidelines should be readily available to educators and students.

3. **Transparency and Explainability:**

○ **The "Black Box" Problem:** Many AI algorithms are complex and opaque, making it difficult to understand how they arrive at decisions. This lack of transparency can erode trust in AI systems and raise concerns about accountability. For example, an AI-powered adaptive learning platform may recommend a specific learning path for a student, but without understanding the rationale behind the recommendation, it's difficult for educators to assess its effectiveness or identify potential biases.

■ **Actionable Tips:**

■ Utilize "explainable AI" (XAI) tools that provide insights into the decision-making processes of AI algorithms. These tools can help educators and students understand how AI arrives at certain recommendations or assessments.

■ Develop clear communication strategies about how AI is used in the learning environment. This includes informing educators and students about the types of data collected, how it is used, and the potential limitations of AI systems.

■ Prioritize human oversight and control over AI-driven recommendations and assessments. Educators should have the autonomy to review and adjust AI-generated recommendations to ensure they align with the learning objectives and individual needs of students.

The Human Element: Why AI Needs a Conductor

While AI offers significant potential in education, it's crucial to remember that it is a tool, not a replacement for human educators. Here's why the human element remains irreplaceable:

- **The Power of Empathy and Social-Emotional Learning:** AI struggles to replicate the human capacity for empathy, understanding, and emotional intelligence. Educators play a vital role in fostering social-emotional learning, building positive relationships with students, and providing personalized support that goes beyond the capabilities of AI.

- **Nurturing Critical Thinking and Problem-Solving Skills:** AI can provide students with information and practice exercises, but it cannot replicate the role of educators in guiding students through the process of critical thinking, analysis, and problem-solving. Educators play a crucial role in helping students develop these essential skills through open-ended discussions, collaborative projects, and real-world applications of knowledge.

- **The Importance of Ethical Judgment and Moral Development:** AI cannot instill ethical values or guide students in making complex moral decisions. Educators play a vital role in fostering ethical development by discussing ethical dilemmas, encouraging critical reflection, and modeling ethical behavior.

Beyond the Ethical: Policy and Regulatory Considerations

The responsible implementation of AI in education requires robust policy and regulatory frameworks. This section explores some key areas that policymakers need to address:

- **Data Governance and Ownership:** Who owns student data collected through AI-powered learning platforms? How can we ensure its responsible use and prevent misuse?

  - Policymakers should develop clear guidelines for data ownership and usage rights. This might involve establishing student data as the property of the student, with clear opt-in and opt-out mechanisms for data collection and use.

    - Strict data security regulations should be implemented to ensure student data is protected from unauthorized access, breaches, and misuse.

  - **Standardization and Interoperability:** With the rapid development of a wide array of AI tools for education, establishing common standards for data collection and exchange becomes crucial.

    - Policymakers can work with educational technology (EdTech) developers to establish standardized data formats and protocols. This ensures data collected by different AI platforms can be easily shared and integrated within a learning ecosystem, promoting data portability and user choice.

- Human Oversight and Control: While AI offers undeniable benefits, it's paramount to ensure human oversight of AI-driven decisions.

  - Policymakers should establish clear guidelines that guarantee human control over AI-powered assessments, recommendations, and curriculum decisions. Educators should have the final say in how AI tools are utilized within their classrooms.

  - Policies should promote transparency regarding AI use in education. This includes informing students and parents about the nature of AI tools used, their limitations, and the recourse available if they have concerns.

- Accountability and Liability: With AI playing a larger role in education, the question of accountability arises. In the case of biased algorithms or inaccurate AI-driven assessments, who is held responsible?

  - Policymakers need to develop frameworks for accountability in AI-powered education. This might involve establishing clear liability structures for EdTech companies and educational institutions in cases of bias, algorithmic errors, or data breaches.

The Global Orchestra: International Considerations for AI in Education

The ethical and regulatory considerations surrounding AI in education extend beyond national borders. As AI tools become more prevalent globally, international collaboration is essential.

- **International Data Sharing Agreements:** The increasing use of cloud-based AI platforms raises concerns about student data crossing international borders.

  - International cooperation is needed to develop data-sharing agreements that ensure student data privacy and security, even when stored or processed across different countries.

- **Global Standards and Best Practices:** There is a need for global collaboration to establish consistent ethical guidelines and best practices for AI development and implementation in education.

  - International organizations such as UNESCO can play a crucial role in facilitating discussions, fostering knowledge sharing, and developing standardized frameworks for ethical AI in education.

The Future Symphony: Embracing AI Responsibly

The future of AI in education holds immense potential. However, responsible implementation requires a commitment to ethical considerations, robust policy frameworks, and ongoing dialogue between educators, policymakers, technology developers, and students.

Reflection for Educators, Students, Policymakers, and Parents:

- **Educators:** Advocate for responsible AI implementation. Seek professional development opportunities to understand AI ethics and best practices. Critically evaluate AI tools before integrating them into your classrooms, prioritizing solutions that align with your teaching philosophy and student needs.

- **Students:** Be informed about how AI is used in your learning environment. Ask questions and express concerns if you feel AI is being used unfairly or in a way that negatively impacts your learning experience.

- **Policymakers:** Develop comprehensive policy frameworks that address data privacy, algorithmic bias, and human oversight in AI-powered education. Focus on promoting transparency, accountability, and responsible data governance practices.

- **Parents:** Educate yourselves about AI in education and its potential implications for your children's learning. Engage in discussions with educators and school administrators about the types of AI tools being used and how they ensure student data privacy and responsible AI use.

Conclusion:

By prioritizing ethical considerations and fostering a collaborative approach, we can ensure that AI becomes a harmonious instrument within the symphony of education. This will empower educators, personalize learning experiences, and ultimately equip all students with the knowledge, skills, and critical thinking abilities necessary to thrive in an AI-driven world.

Reflection Prompts for IT Leaders in Academia: Fostering Responsible AI Integration in Education

The burgeoning landscape of Artificial Intelligence (AI) presents both opportunities and challenges for the academic community. As IT leaders within institutions of higher learning, many folks hold a pivotal position in shaping the responsible implementation of AI tools. Here, a series of carefully curated reflection prompts aims to guide your strategic vision towards the effective and ethical integration of AI within your academic environment.

Strategic Considerations

1. **Aligning with Core Values:** How can AI be strategically leveraged to enhance the learning experiences of our diverse student body, faculty, and staff, while simultaneously upholding the core educational values of equity, accessibility, and fostering critical thinking skills?

2. **Complementing Expertise:** How can we ensure that AI serves as a complementary tool to existing faculty expertise, empowering educators rather than replacing their invaluable roles in the learning process?

3. **Long-Term Vision:** What long-term vision do we have for AI integration within our academic programs and services? How can we leverage AI to cultivate a future-oriented learning environment that prepares students for the evolving demands of the AI-driven world?

Ethical Considerations

1. **Data Governance:** What robust policies and procedures need to be established to safeguard student data privacy and security throughout the entire lifecycle of AI-powered learning platforms and tools within our institution?

2. **Mitigating Bias:** Recognizing the potential for bias within AI algorithms, how can we implement proactive measures to mitigate any algorithmic prejudice that may impact student assessment, personalized learning pathways, or other AI applications?

3. **Transparency in Action:** What strategies can be adopted to maintain a high level of transparency regarding the use of AI in our educational settings? How can we ensure students, faculty, and parents all have a clear understanding of how AI is being implemented and its intended purpose?

4. **Culture of Responsibility:** How can we foster a culture of responsible AI development and implementation within our institution? This encompasses collaborating with faculty and students to ensure ethical considerations are prioritized throughout the entire AI adoption process.

Operational Considerations

1. **Infrastructure Readiness:** What infrastructure upgrades or changes are necessary to provide a robust and secure foundation for the seamless integration of AI tools within our existing technological ecosystem?

2. **Empowering IT Staff:** What resources and training will our IT staff require to effectively manage, support, and troubleshoot AI implementations across the institution?

3. **Cross-Functional Collaboration:** How can we promote a spirit of collaboration between IT, faculty, and other key stakeholders to ensure a smooth and successful adoption of AI in education? This will involve open communication, joint planning efforts, and a shared commitment to achieving positive learning outcomes through AI.

4. **Measuring Impact:** How will we establish robust frameworks to measure the impact and effectiveness of AI-powered educational initiatives on student outcomes and learning objectives? This data-driven approach will guide

future AI investments and ensure we are optimizing AI's contribution to the learning experience.

Collaboration and Advocacy

1. **Faculty Engagement:** How can we effectively collaborate with faculty members to identify potential AI applications that align with their specific teaching objectives and cater to the diverse needs of their students?

2. **Strategic Partnerships:** What partnerships can be established with reputable EdTech companies that prioritize the development and deployment of ethical and reliable AI solutions tailored for the academic environment?

3. **Policy Advocacy:** How can we leverage our leadership role to advocate for the development and implementation of policy frameworks that promote responsible AI use in education, not just at the local and national levels, but also potentially on the international stage?

By engaging in a comprehensive and thoughtful reflection process guided by these prompts, IT leaders in academia can take a proactive approach to shaping the future of AI in education. This leadership will ensure that AI is harnessed as a powerful tool for enhancing learning, fostering innovation, and ultimately promoting a more equitable and effective educational experience for all students within the academic community.

Chapter 9: Global Perspectives and Case Studies in AI and Education: A Learning Symphony Across Borders

Introduction

The global education system is undergoing a significant transformation, largely driven by the integration of Artificial Intelligence (AI). Each nation contributes its distinct approach to what could be described as a worldwide symphony of innovative educational practices. This chapter takes you on a global tour, examining how different countries are leveraging AI to revolutionize their educational systems. We delve into success stories and lessons learned, showcasing how AI fosters a universal shift towards more personalized, effective, and accessible learning solutions.

The First Movement: A Tapestry of National Approaches

AI's integration into education manifests uniquely across different regions, reflecting each country's unique cultural, economic, and technological circumstances.

The Asian Ascendancy

In Asia, countries like South Korea and China are at the forefront of incorporating AI to enhance educational outcomes. South Korea has implemented a national AI tutoring program designed to boost students' skills in critical subjects such as mathematics and science. This program uses adaptive learning algorithms that tailor the difficulty level and pacing of lessons based on individual student performance. This initiative is not just about improving educational outcomes but also about ensuring equitable access to quality education across diverse student populations.

A notable example is the **"AI Tutor"** used in South Korea's public schools, which has been instrumental in providing personalized learning experiences that have led to measurable improvements in student performance in standardized tests (*Source: Ministry of Education, South Korea*).

China, on the other hand, has initiated several AI-powered language learning platforms that specifically cater to the diverse needs of its vast student population. These platforms use AI to create personalized language learning sessions, making it easier for students from different linguistic backgrounds to learn Mandarin. For instance, **iFlytek**, one of China's leading AI firms, has developed technologies that are being used in rural schools to help bridge the language divide between different Chinese dialects (*Source: iFlytek*).

The European Experimentation

Europe takes a cautious yet innovative approach to AI in education, with a focus on ethical practices and maintaining human oversight. Finland and Estonia exemplify this approach by integrating AI into their educational systems to complement traditional teaching methods rather than replace them.

Finland uses AI for formative assessment, where AI systems analyze student submissions to provide teachers with detailed insights that help them tailor their teaching strategies. An example of this is the **"Edu.AI"** project, which aims to develop AI tools that can provide real-time analytics on student learning patterns and help teachers optimize their instructional methods (*Source: Finnish National Agency for Education*).

Estonia, known for its digital innovation, focuses on developing AI tools that support personalized learning pathways, allowing for education that adapts to individual student learning styles and speeds. The **"eKool"** system, an AI-powered tool developed in Estonia, helps track and manage student learning journeys, providing personalized insights and recommendations to educators (*Source: eKool Inc.*).

The American Ambitions

The United States presents a diverse approach to AI in education, characterized by significant private sector involvement and varied adoption levels across public educational institutions. Companies like **Knewton** and **Coursera** are leaders in developing AI-powered educational tools that provide personalized learning experiences across different subjects and educational levels.

However, the widespread adoption of these technologies also raises concerns about data privacy and the potential for algorithmic bias. These challenges have sparked discussions on the need for robust regulatory frameworks to ensure that AI tools are used responsibly and ethically in educational settings. The **"AI and Education Open Project"** led by Stanford University is an initiative aimed at addressing these ethical considerations and promoting transparency and fairness in the use of AI in American schools (*Source: Stanford University*).

Reflection Questions for the Chapter:

- What role should international cooperation play in shaping the future of AI in education?

- How can countries leverage each other's successes and challenges to enhance their own AI integration in education?

- What measures can be taken to ensure that AI in education adheres to global ethical standards while respecting cultural differences?

This detailed exploration into the varied applications of AI across different global contexts provides a comprehensive view of how different educational systems are utilizing technology to enhance learning outcomes and manage challenges. Each section brings to light the unique approaches and considerations that shape the integration of AI in education worldwide.

Chapter 10: The Ethical and Privacy Implications of AI in Education:

Delving Deeper: A Look at Specific Ethical Concerns

While in Chapter 8 focused on Navigating the Symphony's Harmony, there is still more to learn here, with three critical elements:

1. Privacy and Data Security

- Student Data Collection and Use: AI systems require vast amounts of student data, including test scores, learning patterns, and even biometric information (Ferguson, 2022). This raises concerns about the data collected, its intended use, and potential misuse by third parties (Langford, 2020).

Actionable Tips:

- Implement clear data collection policies outlining data types collected, collection purposes, and storage duration (European Commission, 2022).

- Obtain explicit consent from students and parents regarding data collection, ensuring transparency about data usage and anonymization whenever possible (Future of Privacy Forum, 2020).

- Partner with reputable AI vendors prioritizing robust data security measures, including encryption and access controls (AI Now Institute, 2022).

2. Algorithmic Bias and Fairness

- Biased Data Sets: AI algorithms reflect the data they are trained on. Unfortunately, datasets used to train AI systems can perpetuate societal biases (Bostrom & Yudkowsky, 2014). This can lead to unfair assessments, biased learning pathways, and hinder educational opportunities for certain student groups (Crawford, 2021).

Actionable Tips:

- Conduct thorough audits of AI algorithms to identify potential biases in the training data. Collaborate with diversity, equity, and inclusion (DE&I) experts (Gebru et al., 2019).

- Utilize diverse and inclusive datasets reflecting student demographics. This may require actively seeking out data representing various cultures, ethnicities, and learning styles (Mitchell et al., 2019).

- Develop clear guidelines and protocols for mitigating bias in AI-powered education tools readily available to educators and students (OECD, 2019).

3. Transparency and Explainability

- The "Black Box" Problem: Many AI algorithms are complex and opaque, making it difficult to understand how they arrive at decisions (Lipton, 2018). This lack of transparency can erode trust and raise accountability concerns. For example, an AI-powered adaptive learning platform might recommend a specific learning path, but educators struggle to assess its effectiveness or identify potential biases without understanding the rationale behind the recommendation (Selbst et al., 2019).

Actionable Tips:

- Utilize "explainable AI" (XAI) tools that provide insights into AI decision-making processes. These tools can help educators and students understand how AI arrives at certain recommendations or assessments (DARPA, 2020).

- Develop clear communication strategies about AI use in the learning environment. Inform educators and students about data collection types, how it's used, and the potential limitations of AI systems (UNESCO, 2021).

- Prioritize human oversight and control over AI-driven recommendations and assessments. Educators should have the autonomy to review and adjust AI-generated recommendations to ensure alignment with learning objectives and individual student needs (OECD, 2021).

The Human Element: Why AI Needs a Conductor

While AI offers significant potential, it's crucial to remember it's a tool, not a replacement for human educators. Here's why the human element remains irreplaceable:

- The Power of Empathy and Social-Emotional Learning: AI struggles to replicate human empathy, understanding, and emotional intelligence (Brummit, 2020). Educators play a vital role in fostering social-emotional learning, building positive relationships with students, and providing personalized support that goes beyond AI capabilities (CASEL, 2023).

- Nurturing Critical Thinking and Problem-Solving Skills: AI can provide information and practice exercises, but it cannot replicate the role of educators in guiding students through critical thinking, analysis, and problem-solving (Clark et al., 2021). Educators play a crucial role in developing these essential skills through open-ended discussions, collaborative projects, and real-world applications of knowledge (Fredricks et al., 2015).

- The Importance of Ethical Judgment and Moral Development: AI cannot instill ethical values or guide students in making complex moral decisions (Wolt & Berry, 2019). Educators play a vital role in fostering ethical development by discussing ethical dilemmas, encouraging critical reflection, and modeling ethical behavior (National Education Association, 2020).

Beyond the Ethical: Policy and Regulatory Considerations

Responsible AI implementation in education requires robust policy and regulatory frameworks. This section explores key areas policymakers need to address:

- Data Governance and Ownership: Who owns student data collected through

- AI-powered learning platforms? How can we ensure its responsible use and prevent misuse?

Policymakers should:

- Develop clear guidelines for data ownership and usage rights. This might involve establishing student data as the property of the student, with clear opt-in and opt-out mechanisms for data collection and use (Future of Privacy Forum, 2020).

- Implement strict data security regulations to ensure student data is protected from unauthorized access, breaches,and misuse (European Commission, 2022).

- **Standardization and Interoperability:** With the rapid development of a wide array of AI tools for education,establishing common standards for data collection and exchange becomes crucial.

Policymakers can:

- Work with educational technology (EdTech) developers to establish standardized data formats and protocols (OECD, 2020). This ensures data collected by different AI platforms can be easily shared and integrated within a learning ecosystem, promoting data portability and user choice.

- **Human Oversight and Control:** While AI offers undeniable benefits, it's paramount to ensure human oversight of AI-driven decisions.

Policymakers should:

- Establish clear guidelines that guarantee human control over AI-powered assessments, recommendations, and curriculum decisions. Educators should have the final say in how AI tools are utilized within their classrooms (OECD, 2021).

- Develop policies promoting transparency regarding AI use in education. This includes informing students and parents about the nature of AI tools used, their limitations, and the recourse available if they have concerns (UNESCO, 2021).

- **Accountability and Liability:** With AI playing a larger role in education, the question of accountability arises. In the case of biased algorithms or inaccurate AI-driven assessments, who is held responsible?

Policymakers need to:

- Develop frameworks for accountability in AI-powered education. This might involve establishing clear liability structures for EdTech companies and educational institutions in cases of bias, algorithmic errors, or data breaches (AI Now Institute, 2022).

The Global Orchestra: International Considerations for AI in Education

The ethical and regulatory considerations surrounding AI in education extend beyond national borders. As AI tools become more prevalent globally, international collaboration is essential.

- **International Data Sharing Agreements:** The increasing use of cloud-based AI platforms raises concerns about student data crossing international borders.

International cooperation is needed to:

- Develop data-sharing agreements that ensure student data privacy and security, even when stored or processed across different countries (Council of Europe, 2018).

- **Global Standards and Best Practices:** There is a need for global collaboration to establish consistent ethical guidelines and best practices for AI development and implementation in education.

International organizations such as UNESCO can:

- Play a crucial role in facilitating discussions, fostering knowledge sharing, and developing standardized frameworks for ethical AI in education (UNESCO, 2021).

The Future Symphony: Embracing AI Responsibly

The future of AI in education holds immense potential. However, responsible implementation requires a commitment to ethical considerations, robust policy frameworks, and ongoing dialogue between educators, policymakers, technology developers, and students.

Reflection for Educators, Students, Policymakers, and Parents:

Educators:

- Advocate for responsible AI implementation.

- Seek professional development opportunities to understand AI ethics and best practices.

- Critically evaluate AI tools before integrating them into classrooms, prioritizing solutions that align with your teaching philosophy and student needs.

Students:

- Be informed about how AI is used in your learning environment.

- Ask questions and express concerns if you feel AI is being used unfairly or negatively impacts your learning experience.

Policymakers:

- Develop comprehensive policy frameworks that address data privacy, algorithmic bias, and human oversight in AI-powered education.

- Focus on promoting transparency, accountability, and responsible data governance practices.

Parents:

- Educate yourselves about AI in education and its potential implications for your children's learning.

- Engage in discussions with educators and school administrators about the types of AI tools being used and how they ensure student data privacy and responsible AI use.

By working together, we can ensure that AI becomes a powerful force for good in education, empowering educators,personalizing learning experiences, and fostering a future where all students can reach their full potential.

Further Resources:

- Association for Computing Machinery (ACM) - Code of Ethics and Professional Conduct: https://www.acm.org/

- UNESCO - Artificial Intelligence in Education: Mapping the Landscape: https://www.unesco.org/en/digital-education/artificial-intelligence

- Future of Privacy Forum - Student Privacy: https://fpf.org/issue/education/

Epilogue

As we conclude this exploration of AI's transformative impact on education, it is clear that we are only at the beginning of an exciting journey. The potential for AI to revolutionize learning is immense, offering opportunities to create more personalized, efficient, and inclusive educational experiences. However, the path forward requires careful consideration of ethical implications, data privacy, and the irreplaceable value of human educators.

AI should be seen as a tool to augment and enhance the capabilities of teachers, not to replace them. The future of education lies in a harmonious blend of human expertise and AI-driven insights, fostering environments where learners can thrive. As we move forward, let us embrace the possibilities of AI with a commitment to equity, transparency, and continuous improvement. Together, we can shape a future where education is a powerful force for positive change, accessible to all, and capable of unlocking the full potential of every learner.

Testimonials

"In 'AI in Education: An Academic Revolution,' Dr. Levy offers a visionary yet practical guide to the transformative power of AI in education. Her detailed case studies and real-world examples bring theoretical concepts to life, making this book an indispensable tool for researchers and practitioners dedicated to advancing educational technology. Dr. Levy's work sets a new standard in the field."

-- Dr. Anjuli Barnick, Corporate Faculty, Harrisburg University

"Dr. Levy's 'AI in Education: An Academic Revolution' is a groundbreaking exploration of how AI is transforming the educational landscape. Her comprehensive analysis, enriched with historical context and contemporary applications, provides invaluable insights for educators and policymakers alike. This book is a must-read for anyone looking to understand the future of education."

-- Dr. Bahrullah Safi, Chief Strategy Officer, Acacia University

"Dr. Levy masterfully navigates the complexities of AI integration in education, highlighting both its potential and challenges. 'AI in Education: An Academic Revolution' is an essential resource for graduate students and educational leaders aiming to leverage AI to enhance learning outcomes. Her balanced perspective on ethical considerations makes this book a thoughtful and informative read."

-- Stephanie Donofe Meeks, Director Workforce Development, Ashland University

www.ingramcontent.com/pod-product-compliance
Lightning Source LLC
Chambersburg PA
CBHW061830220326
41599CB00027B/5248